7 Laws
OF SPIRITUAL SUCCESS

7 Laws

OF SPIRITUAL SUCCESS

Selwyn Hughes

NOW INCLUDES THE ACCOMPANYING
WORKBOOK BY JENNIFER OLDROYD
***APPLYING THE 7 LAWS
OF SPIRITUAL SUCCESS***

'... let the Holy Spirit unfold for you the basic
laws that govern all spiritual success'

Originally published separately as *The 7 Laws of Spiritual Success* and *Applying the 7 Laws of Spiritual Success* by CWR. *The 7 Laws of Spiritual Success* published 2002 and reprinted 2004, 2005. *Applying the 7 Laws of Spiritual Success* published 2003 and reprinted 2004.

The right of Jennifer Oldroyd to be identified as the author of *Applying the 7 Laws of Spiritual Success* has been asserted by her in accordance with the Copyright, Designs and Patents Act 1988, sections 77 and 78.

This combined edition published 2008 by CWR, Waverley Abbey House, Waverley Lane, Farnham, Surrey GU9 8EP, UK. Registered Charity No. 294387. Registered Limited Company No. 1990308. Reprinted 2008.

See back of book for list of National Distributors.

Unless otherwise indicated, all Scripture references are from the Holy Bible: New International Version (NIV), copyright © 1973, 1978, 1984 by the International Bible Society.

Other Scripture quotations are marked:

AV: The Authorised Version.

NKJV: New King James Version, copyright © 1982, Thomas Nelson Inc.

Phillips: J.B. Phillips: *The New Testament in Modern English*, copyright © 1960, 1972, J.B. Phillips, Fount Paperbacks.

Concept development, editing, design and production by CWR

Cover image: istockphoto, CWR

Printed in Finland by WS Bookwell

ISBN: 978-1-85345-468-4

Contents

Preface

Just after I had celebrated my seventieth birthday on 27 April 1998 I opened up my Bible one morning and my eyes alighted on this verse:

Since my youth, O God, you have taught me,
and to this day I declare your marvellous deeds.
Even when I am old and grey,
do not forsake me, O God,
till I declare your power to the next generation,
your might to all who are to come.

Psa. 71:17–18

The words reverberated in my spirit for days. I just couldn't get away from them. I had the strange feeling that another book was being conceived in my spirit – a book in which I would share with the next generation some of the things God had taught me in the close-on sixty years I had been a Christian.

A sense of urgency seemed to descend upon me, arising I think from the fact that having now crossed the promised 'three score years and ten' and battling with a terminal illness, clearly unless the Lord decides to heal me, I do not have many years left.

Taking a note pad I began to scribble some thoughts. I reflected on the fact that I first came to know Christ as my Saviour whilst a teenager in the valleys of South Wales. I was actually led to the Lord by my uncle, David Thomas, who was also the pastor of the church I attended. He was the man who had taken me in his arms when I was a child of just three weeks and on behalf of my parents had dedicated me to God.

As he prayed, so I have been told, he surprised everyone who was present by ending his prayer of dedication with a passionate and most powerful plea that God would make me a preacher.

It dawned on me as I reflected on that memory that now, seventy years later, my whole life has been the result of a godly pastor's prayer!

Almost immediately after my conversion I felt a yearning to be involved in Christian ministry and at the age of nineteen was called by God to become a preacher. After a period of training in a Bible college I entered the Christian ministry at the age of twenty-two.

As I let my mind run over the years in which I have followed Christ I scribbled these words on my writing pad: 'Selwyn Hughes, you have walked with Christ for more than half a century, in many climes and under many circumstances, often very stumblingly; but what have the years taught you? What have you learned in the time that you have served the Saviour, that can be passed on to the next generation?'

Soon, I had a list of between forty and fifty things which I felt the Lord had taught me – truths which I felt could and should be passed on to the Christians of tomorrow. As I reflected on them, however, I realised that they contained nothing new. Preachers and writers had talked and written about them throughout the whole of the Church age.

The idea lingered with me that perhaps these truths, presented through the medium of my own experience, might come across with a fresh emphasis and be seen in a new light. That certainly is my prayer and the motivation underlying this book.

But forty to fifty concepts would be too many to deal with in one book. It was then that the thought came to me of whittling them down to an irreducible minimum.

What, I asked myself, are the issues that are *absolutely essential* to living an effective and successful Christian life; issues that simply have to be a part of one's daily walk if the Christian life is to work the way it should?

The process of distillation reduced them to seven; less than this I felt one could not go.

A final question arose in my mind: what shall I call these seven key concepts?

Principles?

Beliefs?

Tenets?

Doctrines?

Convictions?

I decided after much reflection to call them 'laws'.

I realise that some might see a reference to 'laws' as somewhat prescriptive and leaning toward legalism. It is possible also that some, having read the title of this book, might be wondering at the wisdom of such a title when Scripture says quite clearly that we are 'not under law but under grace' (Rom. 6:15).

There is great deal of muddled thinking in today's Church about this issue of legalism. I like what Mark Buchanan in his book *Your God is Too Safe* says on the subject:

> *We are overly prone to see legalism lurking behind every exhortation to strive and make an effort to be holy. Every time I say 'work out your salvation', someone will hear me say; 'work for your salvation'. The two are utterly different things.*[1]

Something similar happens whenever the word 'law' or 'laws' is mentioned – we are apt to relate the word to the Ten Commandments and cry 'legalism'. It is not a return to the keeping of the law (the Decalogue) I am referring to in this book but engaging with the spiritual laws that God has built into His kingdom, which in turn enable us to experience more of His power and His presence. The first chapter I think will make this point more clear.

Read on!

Selwyn Hughes, 2002
Waverley Abbey House,
Farnham, Surrey UK

Introduction

'YOU'D BETTER CHANGE COURSE'

A WORLD WITHOUT LAWS? UNIMAGINABLE!

*It is impossible for us to break laws, we only break
ourselves upon them. (Cecil B. De Mille)*

Close on forty years ago an event took place in my life that launched me on a voyage of discovery for which I have never ceased to be thankful.

It happened in the mid-1960s when I invited Bob Stewart, a young scientist, to be a dinner guest in my home. I was a pastor in central London at the time and my wife and I thought that Bob, being single, a newcomer to the city and a recent member of my church, might enjoy an evening with our family.

Within a few minutes of sitting down to a delicious meal prepared by my wife he said, 'I want you to tell me if in your work as a pastor and counsellor you have discovered laws working in the personality as certain and reliable as those we scientists see at work in the material universe?'

'Why do you ask?' I enquired.

He hesitated for a moment, then said, 'Because it seems the more I understand the Bible and relate to people, the more convinced I am that the great lines running through the universe which we call "laws" do not stop at what scientists call "the natural sphere", but are to be observed in the spiritual sphere also.'

That led to an interesting dinner conversation.

I am afraid I did not have much to contribute as the idea was quite new to me, but what we discussed around the table that evening triggered in me a strong desire to explore the subject as fully as possible.

NATURAL LAWS

A book that helped me more than any other was Professor Henry Drummond's *Natural Law in the Spiritual World*. It is a book full of the germs and seeds of things and I found it a trustworthy guide as I sought to understand the concept of laws being present not only in the natural world but also in the spiritual world.

Among many interesting things, Henry Drummond made the point that the whole concept of natural laws is something that has emerged only in the past few hundred years.

I found this paragraph particularly illuminating:

> *In the earlier centuries, before the birth of science, Phenomena were studied alone. The world then was a chaos, a collection of single, isolated, and independent facts. Deeper thinkers saw, indeed, that relations must subsist between these facts, but the Reign of Law was never more to the ancients than a far-off vision ... With Copernicus, Galileo and Kepler the first regular lines of the universe began to be discerned. When Nature yielded to Newton her great secret ... the pursuit of law became the passion of science ... Newton did not discover Gravity – that is not discovered yet. He discovered its Law, which is Gravitation, but that tells us nothing of its origin, of its nature, or of its cause.*[1]

Revealing words which led me to think: what kind of world would it be without natural laws? As I pondered this issue I tried to imagine a universe where everything happened not by law but by chance; where the sun might rise or it might not; where if someone jumped up in the air he or she might never come down again; where the moon might come out in the middle of the day; where today a child's body might be so light it would float to the ceiling and tomorrow so heavy that it might crash through the floor.

These thoughts are expanded in a book I remember reading as a child entitled *The Chance World*. I have tried in vain to trace it in recent years but have been unsuccessful. It told of children being born with two heads, of cement setting one day within seconds and on other occasions taking years to solidify. Every day antecedent and consequent varied and everything changed from hour to hour. This is what the world would be like without laws.

The laws of nature are great lines that run through the universe reducing it like parallels of latitude to intelligent order. They are simply the statements of the orderliness of things and sustain what God has put in motion. But the issue I began to wrestle with back there in the early 1960s was this: do these lines stop with what we call the natural sphere?

Is it not possible that they might lead further? Did the hand that established them give up the work where most of all they were required?

SPIRITUAL LAWS

Now, after working as a pastor and a counsellor for over fifty years, I am convinced that the Creator built into the human personality spiritual laws that are as sure, certain and reliable as those we have discovered in the natural realm.

The apostle Paul introduces us to one of these spiritual laws in his epistle to the Romans. Here's what he says:

> *Therefore, there is now no condemnation for those who are in Christ Jesus, because through Christ Jesus the law of the Spirit of life set me free from the law of sin and death.*
>
> Rom. 8:1–2

When talking to groups I have often illustrated this thought of the apostle's by holding a book on the palm of my hand and saying, 'There is a law – a law of gravity – trying to pull this book to the floor. Why doesn't it fall?' The answer is of course that a stronger law – the law of suspension operating through my hand is in those circumstances stronger than the law of gravity. One law supersedes the other.

THE POWER OF THE HOLY SPIRIT

The law of the Spirit of life, the controlling power of the Holy Spirit – who is life-giving – is stronger in the believer than the controlling power of sin which ultimately produces death.

How many occasions have we had in our lives to be grateful for the controlling power of the Holy Spirit working in us to counter the downward effects of the law of sin?

Where would I have been, where would *you* have been but for the blessed Holy Spirit? At our first foolish fingering with sin, as soon as sin seduced our hearts and inflamed our desires, when our vagrant wishes tried to run after sensual images; if He had not been there to sustain and support us, where would we have been?

How grateful ought every Christian to be for the Holy Spirit who is at work within us pleading against the sinful desires with which every one of us is acquainted. A verse from one of Charles Wesley's hymns refers to the work of the Spirit in this way:

Christ is our Advocate on high,
Thou art our Advocate within;
O plead the truth and make reply
To every argument of sin.

But He not only pleads against every argument of sin, He breaks its power and hold over us. If we let Him, of course.

LAWS OF THE SOUL

The idea Bob Stewart dropped into my mind that there may be laws working in the human personality as sure and reliable as the laws in the natural universe settled in my mind as an 'apperception thought'.

This is a term used a lot by psychologists. If it is new to you then this is what it's all about. An 'apperception thought' is a powerful notion or idea that establishes itself in your mind and around which other similar ideas and thoughts easily encrust.

It works like this. Let's say your present car is falling to bits and you decide it's time to invest in a new model. During a visit to a showroom you fall in love with a certain type of car that seems perfect for you. When the salesman says, 'You would look good in that' your mind is made up. Though it's a little beyond your price range you are determined that you are going to make every effort to purchase it.

You begin to think about it at every spare moment. You even dream about it. You visualise yourself being the proud owner of it and you find that as you drive around the town or the area in which you live you become aware of an amazing thing – almost every third or fourth car you see is the model you have set your heart upon.

The truth is of course that those particular models were there in the same numbers before, but you hadn't noticed them. Now, however, an 'apperception thought' has established itself in your mind and becomes a magnet to which all things similar attach themselves.

The 'apperception thought' Bob Stewart dropped into my mind that day around my dinner table, about the possibility of laws being present in the personality, began to work for me in some astonishing ways in the counselling room.

I was always aware, of course, that there were certain principles at work in people's lives, but the deeper I looked into the souls of men and women the more I saw that such things merited a much stronger label than 'principles'; they deserved the classification of 'laws'.

I began to notice, for example, that when someone chose not to forgive offences done to them it followed as the night the day that the consequences of not forgiving brought inner disruption and disease. There were no exceptions. When resentment and bitterness remain in the soul then degeneration takes place as surely as a garden is overrun by weeds when it is not tended.

Sometimes the inner disruption would not manifest itself outwardly but it was there all the time, undermining the very structure of the soul. It is a law as reliable as the law of gravity.

In the chapters that follow I will talk more about the laws that I have discovered working in the soul and will introduce you to what I consider to be the seven basic laws that, when followed, lead to spiritual and personal success.

Some, I realise, will see the words 'principle' and 'law' as synonymous terms. I offer no argument against that view. I think however that the word 'law' carries with it stronger connotations than the word 'principle' and also, as I am drawing comparisons from the world of natural laws, 'law' seems the right word to use.

WHY LAWS?

A law, says my dictionary, 'is a statement of scientific truth that is invariable under given conditions'. It goes on to describe a whole list of laws such as the law of cause and effect, the law of supply and demand, the law of the jungle, the law of large numbers, the law of diminishing returns, the law of averages and so on.

One that I found intriguing as a counsellor is the law of parsimony – the rule that simple explanations should be preferred to more complicated ones and that new phenomena should be based on what is already known.

Time and time again when dealing with people's problems I have followed this law and found it to be a most helpful approach. I can't tell you the number of times I have had people come to me having been diagnosed as demon-possessed, only to find that the bizarre symptoms they manifested could easily and adequately be explained, not by demonic control or influence, but by the indulgence of the carnal nature.

The simple explanation I found was the right one. That is not to say there are no genuine cases of demonic possession, but in my experience they are few and far between.

Although I am not a scientist (my secular training was in the field of engineering) I have always been fascinated by what little I know about natural laws. And what captivates me about them is their certainty and reliability.

In chemistry, for example, H_2O produces water. We may disagree with this formula, fight with it and try to twist it into something else, but in the end we will have to surrender to it, accept it, obey it – or we will not produce water. Two parts of hydrogen and one of oxygen is the way and everything else is not-the-way.

It is the same in the air. There is a way to fly and there is a way not-to-fly. Those wishing to fly must obey the laws upon which flying depends.

Dr E. Stanley Jones in his book *The Way* says:

*There can be no moral holidays in the air. You obey or be broken. You gain
mastery only by obedience. Aviation did not invent those laws or impose
them; it discovered them.*[2]

This necessity of obedience to laws holds good not only in the
material universe but also, as we shall see, in the matter of human living.
Chance does not reign here any more than it does in the material universe.
You can't do as you please and get away with it.

There is something built into the human constitution that says,
'Obey and you get results; disobey and you get consequences.' Is that
something which demands obedience merely a set of conventions and
customs, or is it written into the nature of reality?

Emmanuel Kant, the philosopher, while reflecting on these same
matters said, 'Two things astonish me; the starry heavens above and the
moral law within.' E. Stanley Jones poses this question in relation to Kant's
remarks: 'Did he mean that the laws of those two worlds are equally
dependable and equally authoritative and equally inescapable?'

Well, we don't know exactly what was in Kant's mind when he made
that remark but the answer to the question of whether the two worlds are
equally dependable must surely be 'Yes'. There is something in this
universe that has the last word, no matter who has the first word.

Many people do not believe that there is a last word. In a television
programme I saw recently some young people were talking about cheating
and stealing and one of them, when asked if he thought it was OK to do
that, replied, 'It's OK to do these things as long as you can get away with it.'

But nobody gets away with anything in a moral universe.

Dr Cynddylan Jones, a famous Welsh preacher, used to say, 'The
worst thing about doing wrong is to be the one who does the wrong.'

I don't know about you, but I used to think that the text 'Be sure your sin will find you out' (Num. 32:23), meant 'Be sure your sin will be found out'. It doesn't say that, however. It says your sin will find *you* out. It will register in you, demean you, make you less of a person and, if it continues, there will be deterioration and decay.

In the television programme one of the young men being interviewed said, 'I love this guy called "Kick"… I want him to be a partner in my life.' I thought to myself that there is another guy that follows hard on his heels called 'Kick Back' – and he always has the last kick.

We may be free to choose but we are not free to choose the consequences of our choosing. The universe always has the last word.

Phyllis Bottome in a book called *Survival* says:

> *We must not try to manipulate life; rather we must try to find out what life demands of us and train ourselves to fulfil these demands. It is a long and humbling business.*

Wise words. Yet many are trying to do just that – manipulate life. They demand of life instead of listening to what life demands of them. And the results are written in frustration and wreckage.

If you won't be humble then you will be humbled.

Obeying law, whether it is in the natural or the spiritual, leads to successful living in this world. In obeying law you get its benefits; when you disobey it you get its consequences.

I have always loved this story which I came across many years ago in the *Reader's Digest*. It happened to a man by the name of Frank Koch and was first told in *Proceedings*, the magazine of the American Naval Institute.

Two battleships assigned to the training squadron had been at sea on manoeuvres in heavy weather for several days. I was serving on the lead battleship and was on watch on the bridge as night fell. The visibility was poor, with patchy fog, so the captain remained on the bridge keeping an eye on all activities. Shortly after dark, the lookout on the wing of the bridge reported, 'Light bearing on the starboard bow.'

'Is it steady or moving astern?' the captain called out.

Lookout replied, 'Steady, captain,' which meant we were on a dangerous collision course with that ship.

The captain then called to the signalman, 'Signal that ship: "We are on a collision course. Advise you change course 20 degrees." '

Back came a signal: 'Advisable for you to change course 20 degrees.'

The captain said, 'Send: "I'm a captain. Change course 20 degrees." '

'I'm a seaman second class,' came the reply. 'You had better change course 20 degrees.'

By that time, the captain was furious. He spat out, 'Send this message: "I'm a battleship. Change course 20 degrees." '

Back came the flashing light: 'I'm a lighthouse.'

We changed course.

GOD'S LIGHTHOUSE

The laws of God both in the natural and spiritual sphere are like lighthouses. They cannot shift and cannot change. As Cecil B. De Mille observed in his film *The Ten Commandments*, 'It is impossible for us to break laws; we only break ourselves upon them.'

The lighthouse laws that govern human growth and happiness are woven into the fabric of our society and comprise the roots of every family and institution that has endured and prospered.

The same moral law which God has revealed in Scripture He has also stamped on human nature. He has in fact written His law twice, once in the text of the Bible and once in the texture of human nature; once on stone tablets and once on human hearts.

The moral law is not an alien system which it is unnatural for people to obey; it fits perfectly as a hand into a glove, because it is the law of our own created being. There is a fundamental correspondence between God's law in the Bible and the one written on our hearts. We can discover our true humanness by obeying it.

Before concluding this opening chapter I have one more thing I want to do and that is to define what I mean by 'spiritual success'.

TRUE SUCCESS

Many Christians feel the word 'success' has a slightly worldly connotation. An American publisher when asked the question, 'What sells?' replied, 'Anything with the word "success" in it.'

Everybody, especially in the realms of business, commerce or politics, wants to be successful but there is a great difference between the way the world sees success and the way God sees it.

I like what Luci Shaw says about success:

I believe that a measure of success is essential in the formulae for human living. But the more I think about it, the more I am convinced that succeeding (in the commonest sense of that word) may be either destructive or healthy, depending on what motivates it. Our culture always urges us to do better, to be competitive, to win the pennant, to take home the biggest Christmas bonus, to pick up a Pulitzer or at least to raise the most self-confident children. Such success is nearly always pride and ambition centred. And it's addictive. Achievers need a regular 'success' fix.[3]

Does the Bible use the concept of success? Most definitely. The word 'success' and its synonyms, appears many times in Scripture. Here are just a few:

Do not let this Book of the Law depart from your mouth; meditate on it day and night, so that you may be careful to do everything written in it. Then you will be prosperous and successful.

Josh. 1:8

He [Uzziah] sought God during the days of Zechariah, who instructed him in the fear of God. As long as he sought the LORD, God gave him success.

2 Chron. 26:5

So he sent David away from him and gave him command over a thousand men, and David led the troops in their campaigns. In everything he did he had great success, because the LORD was with him.

1 Sam. 18:13–14

What did God have in mind when He said He would give His servants success? It meant of course that God would bless the work of their hands, but God had in mind soul prosperity, too.

What good is success in material things if the soul does not prosper?

That great Old Testament character, Joseph, in spite of much that was against him, climbed the ladder of success, rising from a prisoner with a few privileges to the Keeper of the Royal Seal and authority second only to the throne.

I have met many people in my time who are successful by this world's standards – they have money, wealth, fame, popularity – but inwardly they are beggared and bankrupt.

And I have to say also that in my many years of ministry I have come across a good number of Christians who are incredibly successful in terms of their professional life, but not in terms of their personal life.

One Bible college I know had this as its motto: 'To be in God's will is better than success.' Years later, after a number of students debated the issue, it was changed to: 'To be in God's will is success.'

I have come to the conclusion after years of thought on this subject that success in a Christian sense is this: knowing the will of God and doing it.

But how do we know when we are in the centre of God's will? Well, one way is by searching His Word, the Bible, obeying that Word and living according to the laws which God has laid down in His universe for the development of our characters.

Be sure of this, no one can be truly successful if he or she is not a person of character. I like what David Starr Jordan wrote: 'There is no real excellence in all this world which can be separated from right living.'

Listen to what one writer, a professional businessman, says on this point:

If I try to use human influence, strategies and tactics of how to get other people to do what I want to, to work better, to be more motivated, to like me and each other – while my character is fundamentally flawed, marked by duplicity and insincerity – then in the long run, I cannot be successful. My duplicity will breed distrust and everything I do – even using so-called good human relations techniques – will be perceived as manipulative. It simply makes no difference how good the rhetoric is, or even how good the intentions are; if there is little or no trust, there is no foundation for permanent success. Our basic goodness gives life to technique.[4]

Spiritual success does not just happen. I saw this on a poster outside a church in Los Angeles many years ago:

> *S_ CCESS – what's missing?*
> *Even God can't spell*
> *S_CCESS without U*

The point the poster was making I think is that success is a combination of God and you. You need God and He needs you. It's a team effort. You can't do it without Him and He won't do it without you.

He will give himself fully to us providing we give ourselves fully to Him by depending on His Spirit and obeying His Word.

The only way you can have success in your Christian life is when you follow His commandments and obey His Word.

I have heard people pray, 'O Lord, make me a success.' And they expect Him to do it without any contribution from them. As I said, success in spiritual terms does not just happen. You have to team up with God.

Malcolm Muggeridge in his book, *A 20th Century Testimony*, said:

When I look back on my life nowadays, which I sometimes do, what strikes me most forcibly about it is that what seemed at the time most significant and seductive seems now the most futile and absurd. For instance success in all of its various guises; being known and being praised; ostensible pleasures like acquiring money or seducing women, or travelling, going to and fro in the world and up and down in it like

Satan, exploring and experiencing whatever Vanity Fair has to offer. In retrospect all these exercises in self-gratification seem pure fantasy, what Pascal called 'licking the earth'.[5]

I said earlier that I am not a scientist. Life, however, has forced me to become a Christian scientist. By that I mean someone who has studied and gained a healthy respect for the laws of the soul, those laws which when obeyed lead to healthy and successful living. But what are these spiritual laws that lead to successful living? How can they be identified? And are there just seven?

No, but in my judgment the seven spiritual laws I write about in this book are the most basic of these and an inability or an unwillingness to recognise them and live by them leads in turn to unsuccessful living.

Sit down with me at the foot of the cross and let the Holy Spirit unfold for you the basic laws that govern all spiritual effectiveness and success.

Law 1
FIRST THINGS FIRST

MAKE WORSHIP YOUR FIRST FOCUS

Things which matter most must never be at the mercy
of things which matter least. (Goethe)

It happened in the year 1961. A group of ministers were gathered together in a town in Canada for a few days of conference and to hear a pastor from an inconspicuous church on the south side of Chicago. His name was Aiden Wilson Tozer. He preferred to be known simply as A.W. Tozer.

Tozer began his series of messages with these words: 'I want to talk to you in these next few days about what I believe is the missing jewel of the evangelical church.'

As he paused, everyone wondered what it would be. Evangelism? Prayer? Witnessing? Social action? No. 'The missing jewel in the evangelical church,' he said, 'is worship.'

From that opening moment to the close of the conference A.W. Tozer held those men spellbound as he expounded the theme of worship. So helpful were those messages that they were put together into a booklet that is still available today, as indeed are most of Tozer's works.

OUR WEAKEST AREA

As I write, four decades have passed since Tozer made that statement but that jewel is still largely missing both corporately and individually in the contemporary Christian Church.

Robert Webber of Wheaton College, USA, in the Foreword to a book called *Praise! A Matter of Life and Breath* by Ronald Barclay Allen, said:

> *Worship is the weakest area of evangelical Christianity. We are strongest in the areas of evangelism, teaching and fellowship. We are improving*

greatly in the area of servanthood (application of the Gospel to social needs) and the ministry of healing (counselling and caring for the emotional needs of people) but depth in the area of worship is badly lacking. We hardly know where to begin because we have lost nearly all contact with the past.[1]

Robert Webber is of course talking about corporate worship here and although there are some churches where the 'jewel' sparkles and shines, they are, it must be said, few and far between.

As a preacher I have found myself in many different kinds of churches and a common complaint I hear is this: 'Our pastor (or leader) is a wonderful Bible teacher who opens up the Scriptures for us in the most amazing ways, but our church has no sense of worship.'

Charles Swindoll says that as he has gone into different churches he has noticed that a strong pulpit often means weakness in worship.

One of the most surprising and incisive comments I think I have ever heard in relation to worship came from someone in a charismatic church who said, 'We have good preaching here, good music and good services; everything always has to be upbeat. But we are so preoccupied with praising God that we have no time to worship Him.'

WORSHIP, NOT JUST PRAISE

Perhaps at this stage I ought to make clear the difference between the words 'worship' and 'praise' as some see them as synonymous terms.

Praise is appreciating God for what He does; worship is adoring Him for who He is.

C.S. Lewis, with his characteristic lucidity, put it like this: 'I learned how a thing can be revered, not for what it can do to us, but for what it is in itself.' It was then, he said, that he understood the difference between praise and worship.

Although many good things have happened in our churches in the past few decades, generally speaking we are still fairly ignorant of what worship really means.

Worship is not just praising God but being in awe of Him, adoring Him – not for what He gives but for who He is. Strictly speaking, in worship there is no prayer or intercession. It is gazing on God in love and adoring Him just for Himself. Christians who know this experience can think of no bliss in eternity which will exceed the bliss of gazing on Him. They say with Faber:

> *Father of Jesus, love's reward,*
> *What rapture it will be,*
> *Prostrate before thy throne to lie*
> *And gaze and gaze on Thee!*

But it is not so much with corporate worship I am concerned here; rather it is with individual worship. I am thinking of it in the way that Jesus used the word when tempted by the devil in the wilderness:

> *Again, the devil took him to a very high mountain and showed him all the kingdoms of the world and their splendour. 'All this I will give you,' he said, 'if you will bow down and worship me.' Jesus said to him, 'Away from me, Satan! For it is written: "Worship the Lord your God, and serve him only."' '*

Matt. 4:8–10

Our Lord was offered all the kingdoms of the world if He would bow down and worship Satan. The Saviour's answer is clear and unequivocal: God is the only one to be worshipped.

OUR FIRST RESPONSIBILITY

The first responsibility of every Christian is to worship God. *It is, I believe, the first law of the soul.* When we violate that law we put our souls in peril.

When Jesus said, 'It is written: "Worship the Lord your God, and serve him only" ' He was referring to the statement originally found in Deuteronomy 6:13; but there are many other biblical texts that carry the same message.

In fact Scripture fairly bulges with the truth that God is to be the first and only object of our worship. From Genesis to Revelation the emphasis cannot be missed – God commands us to worship Him. Nothing, absolutely nothing is more important than this.

Do you know the first reference to worship in the Bible? This might surprise you. You can read about it in Genesis 22 when Abraham is about to sacrifice his son Isaac on the altar. At the foot of the mountain and before they began their ascent Abraham says to his servants:

> *'Stay here with the donkey while I and the boy go over there. We will worship and then we will come back to you.'*
>
> (v.5)

And do you know the last reference to worship in Scripture? It is found in the final chapter of the last book – the book of Revelation. Strikingly this is what it says:

'I am a fellow-servant with you and with your brothers the prophets and of all who keep the words of this book. Worship God!'

Rev. 22:9

One of the oldest books in the Bible is the book of Job. You know the story, but as a reminder let's look at part of the opening chapter. Satan came before God and said about this God-fearing man:

'Does Job fear God for nothing? ... Have you not put a hedge around him and his household and everything he has? You have blessed the work of his hands, so that his flocks and herds are spread throughout the land. But stretch out your hand and strike everything he has, and he will surely curse you to your face.' The LORD *said to Satan, 'Very well, then, everything he has is in your hands, but on the man himself do not lay a finger.' Then Satan went out from the presence of the* LORD.

Job 1:9–12

Satan got to work and one day, like a bolt out of the blue, tidings of disaster come crashing in upon Job. Hot on the heels of one another come the messengers of woe. The reports are desolating: his oxen and asses have gone, his sheep and camels are gone, his servants are gone, his children are gone.

With a single stroke he is bereft of almost everything. But think of the moral splendour of this: the patriarch, hearing the numbing news, falls down on the ground and – *worships* (v.20). How many modern-day followers of the Almighty would have done that?

So what does it mean to worship God in a personal and individual sense?

DESIGNED FOR WORSHIP

Deep within every heart is a desire to worship God. This is because in the beginning God designed us for worship. The primary purpose behind the creation of mankind was that we might freely and intelligently worship the Creator.

The Westminster Catechism asks the question: 'What is the chief end of man?' and answers it in this way: 'The chief end of man is to glorify God and enjoy him for ever.' Only when this truth is understood and practised will our souls function in the way they were designed.

One of the failures of modern-day Christians is to put work before worship. We take our converts and immediately set about making workers out of them. God never meant it to be so. God meant that every convert should learn first how to worship Him and only after that become a worker.

God is not primarily in the business of recruiting labourers for His harvest field. His chief aim is to restore fallen men and women to the condition where they can offer Him true worship.

Our Lord made this point clear to the Samaritan woman at the well of Sychar:

> *'Yet a time is coming and has now come when the true worshippers will worship the Father in spirit and truth, for they are the kind of worshippers the Father seeks.'*
>
> John 4:23

And then He adds this pungent statement:

> *'God is spirit, and his worshippers must worship in spirit and in truth.'*
>
> John 4:24

Those whose main work is in the field of evangelism need not be frightened of this emphasis that worship must come first and work second, for labour and service that do not flow out of a worshipping heart will appear only as wood, hay and stubble in the day when everyone's work is tried.

No one can worship God for long without seeing and sensing the need to work for Him. A vision of God such as Isaiah experienced in the temple leads ultimately to the obligation of service becoming too strong to resist. The true worshipper responds as Isaiah did: 'Here am I. Send me!' (Isa. 6:8).

WORSHIP BEFORE WORK

Nowhere is the truth that God wants us to be worshippers first and workers second more clear than in the story of Martha and Mary as recorded in Luke's Gospel chapter 10:

> But Martha was distracted by all the preparations that had to be made. She came to him and asked, 'Lord, don't you care that my sister has left me to do the work by myself? Tell her to help me!'
>
> 'Martha, Martha,' the Lord answered, 'you are worried and upset about many things, but only one thing is needed. Mary has chosen what is better, and it will not be taken away from her.'
>
> Luke 10:40–42

Martha, bustling about her domestic duties in the home, thought the priority at that moment was her work. Mary thought otherwise. Our Lord, who was always able to distinguish between the urgent and the important, made the point well when he said to Martha, 'Mary has chosen the better thing.'

Our work for God is important, but not so important as our worship of Him. It is tragic when we become more interested in the work of God than in God Himself; more taken up with the cause of Christ than with the Christ whose cause we represent.

Don Bjork of Worldteam points out that the great commission was given to worshipping people, for Matthew records, 'They worshipped him' (Matt. 28:17). He reminds us that it was while they were worshipping that our Lord said:

> *'Therefore go and make disciples of all nations, baptising them in the name of the Father and of the Son and of the Holy Spirit, and teaching them to obey everything I have commanded you. And surely I am with you always, to the very end of the age.'*
>
> Matt. 28:19

A LOVING RELATIONSHIP

How true it is that unless we are involved with Jesus Christ in a loving and adoring relationship we have nothing of eternal value to offer a dying world.

We must come to a definite conclusion about this before we move any further. Our work for God must flow out of our worship. No exceptions, no rationalisations. Nothing must take the place of our first obligation, the first law of the soul, *the worship of God*.

Before we can reach the world we must be committed to reaching God. Our greatest danger is the one which Martha illustrates for us – allowing the urgent to crowd out the important. After all, it is not God who loads us with the tasks that bend and break us. These come from our inner compulsions, coupled with the pressure of circumstances.

We must learn to differentiate between the urgent and the important and make the adoration and worship of God our life's number one priority.

I do not want to overlook the fact that our work for God can be an act of worship. Paul reminds us:

> *Therefore, I urge you, brothers, in view of God's mercy, to offer your bodies as living sacrifices, holy and pleasing to God – this is your spiritual act of worship.*

Rom. 12:1

Clearly then we can worship God with our bodies. When we teach a class of children, sing in the choir, play an instrument, give out books, steward and see people to their seats, drive someone to church, take a hot meal to an old or infirm person, visit the sick – we can make all these deeds acts of worship if they are done as unto the Lord.

We can worship as we work, but the thought I am trying to get across here is the necessity of developing an attitude of soul, the atmosphere of one's spirit, a holy sense of awe that one lives and moves and has one's being in God.

Unless there is in the soul the atmosphere of devotion, then our work – however spiritual it might appear – is not an act of worship.

I was reading through Paul's epistle to the Romans the other day. It's a book I have read hundreds of times over the years, but what struck me on this occasion was the way in which Paul, after dealing with the most taxing theology in Romans 11, suddenly lifts his heart in direct worship of God:

> *Oh, the depth of the riches of the wisdom and knowledge of God!*
> *How unsearchable his judgments,*

and his paths beyond tracing out!

'Who has known the mind of the Lord?

Or who has been his counsellor?'

'Who has ever given to God,

that God should repay him?'

For from him and through him and to him are all things.

To him be the glory for ever! Amen.

Rom. 11:33–36

Paul was a worshipping man. Everywhere in his letters he lifts up his heart in worship and praise to God. It must have been while Paul was worshipping that he was caught up into the third heavens (2 Cor. 12).

'Worship,' said someone, 'is what makes a saint.' And there was no greater saint than Paul the apostle.

One of my favourite passages of Scripture that illustrates the priority of worship can be found tucked away in the first book of Kings. It has to do with the construction of the temple where Solomon tells us that the walls of the inner and outer courts were covered in pure gold. And on those golden, gleaming walls, he tells us were 'carved figures of cherubim, palm trees, and open flowers' (1 Kings 6:29, NKJV).

For years I wondered what was behind the symbolism of the carved figures of cherubim, palm trees and open flowers. Then one day it dawned on me. The cherubim are the symbol of *worship*; the palm tree, because of its usefulness (it has 360 uses, says my encyclopaedia) is the symbol of *work*; and the open flowers are the symbol of *witness*, spreading the sweet perfume of the loveliness of God's presence wherever we go.

But notice the first on the list – the cherubim.

Some would argue that something has to be first and there is really no priority intended here. I disagree. I believe the Holy Spirit, who inspired Solomon in the construction of the temple, wanted the cherubim to be first on this list in order to emphasise the priority of worship.

Everywhere you come across the cherubim in Scripture you will see them engaged in worship. Their very existence spells out the fact that they are there to worship God. And why? Because that is the *primary* reason for our existence here on planet Earth.

Let us be quite clear about this: the first reason for us being here in the world is not to preach, teach, counsel, organise church services or sell books. However good these things may be, the primary reason for our existence is to worship God. God wants us first and foremost to worship Him. Nothing can be more important than that.

This fact has been emphasised by theologians down the ages. From Augustine to John Stott, from Anselm to Jim Packer, they have all said the same: worship should be the first occupation of the Christian soul.

WHY WORSHIP?

Why does God want us to worship Him? What lies behind this command of the Almighty that He is to be our first and full focus? There was a time during my student days when I used to puzzle over the thought that God commands us to worship Him. I wondered whether God was egotistical and wanted worship in the same way that a self-centred person or someone with a low self-image is always fishing for compliments.

It was C.S. Lewis who put me right on this. In what I consider is one of the richest passages in all his writings I read this:

> *He is that Object to admire (or, if you like, to appreciate) which is simply to be awake, to have entered the real world; not to appreciate which is*

to have lost the greatest experience and in the end to have lost all. The incomplete and crippled lives of those who are tone-deaf, have never been in love, never known true friendship, never cared for a good book, never enjoyed the feel of the morning air on their cheeks, never (I am one of these) enjoyed football are faint images of it ...

It is in the process of being worshipped that God communicates His presence to men. The miserable idea that God should in any sense need or crave our worship like a vain woman wanting compliments or a vain author presenting his new books to people who have never met or heard of him is implicitly answered by the words: 'If I be hungry I will not tell thee.' Even if such an absurd deity could be conceived He would hardly come to us, the lowest of rational creatures, to gratify His appetite. I don't want my dog to bark approval of my books.[2]

Lewis's thought that in the process of being worshipped God communicates His presence to us revolutionised my thinking on this subject. I saw that when we open in our hearts the door of worship God comes through that door and gives Himself to us. We are the beneficiaries of worship, not Him.

A counsellor I know, and someone who is a personal friend, Dr Larry Crabb, believes that most problems arise in the personality as a result of our failure truly to worship God.

I have noticed in my own counselling experience that whenever I talked to people with deep emotional problems and asked them what the word 'worship' means to them, they look at me blankly and say, 'I am not sure.'

After hundreds of hours in the counselling room exploring this issue I came to see that underlying many emotional problems was a defensive attitude towards trust.

NO TRUST – NO WORSHIP

It was the great Christian writer Oswald Chambers who said, 'The root of sin is the suspicion that God is not good.' If we carry in our hearts any doubts about the goodness of God and allow those doubts to grow to a degree where they harden into a constant suspicion of God's goodness, then we will be unable to worship.

And why? Because it is not possible to worship a God you do not trust.

This is why many Christians can stand up with the rest of the congregation and sing songs of praise, but they cannot enter into true worship. They may mouth the words, but in their heart of hearts they cannot worship; for they find it difficult to trust God.

Often the argument is raised that because people have been hurt and let down by the significant others in their lives – and, let's face it, some people have been badly traumatised by the failure of others to come through for them – this accounts for their inability to trust God.

In my experience, however, the inability to trust is often fuelled by a refusal to trust, and unless this is faced and dealt with there can be no real progress in the soul.

I wonder if this is what C.S. Lewis had in mind when he referred to worship as 'inner health made audible'? There can be no true health in the soul where the soul does not give itself to God in absolute worship.

One of the reasons I believe people who have psychological problems find it difficult to worship is because they are bound so much by their ego. I often tell my students when talking to them about counselling that one of my favourite definitions of the counselling process is this: releasing people to better and more effectively worship God.

Unless this issue of confidence in God as a good and trustworthy Being is established in the soul, worship becomes impossible.

One bestseller in recent years was the book written by Rabbi Kushner entitled *When Bad Things Happen to Good People*.[3] The good Rabbi went through a bitter experience when his son was afflicted with a disease which produced in him a state of premature ageing.

At eighteen he looked like a man of eighty. He died when he was nineteen and the Rabbi, wanting to console his own soul, tried to think through why God allowed bad things to take place in the lives of those who attempt to live good, respectable lives.

He concluded that while God's heart remains ever beneficent, the presence of sin in the universe has brought about a limitation to His power, so that while He wills good He is, in some cases, powerless to prevent evil.

That seemed to solve the problem, but it did it in such a way that denied the omnipotence of God. Christians believe that God is not only good but also all-powerful. Although we can come up with some reasons why God allows bad things to happen to good people (free will, allowing the bad because it can be turned to greater good, and so on) ultimately it is a matter of trust.

Christians are called to trust God when they cannot trace Him and to believe that whatever He allows which we may describe as bad is part of a purpose which we cannot fully understand now but that one day we will. Until that day dawns we trust.

If there is no trust in the soul there will be no true worship for, as I said earlier, it is difficult to worship God when you are not sure you can trust Him.

A RIGHT VIEW OF GOD

The concept we hold of God in our hearts is crucial to the way we will worship Him.

For example, take the case of Dr Joseph Cooke, a brilliant anthropologist and one-time missionary to Thailand. He experienced a breakdown on the mission field and had to return home to the United States. Following his recovery he came to see that part of his problem arose because of a faulty view of God. In his book, *Free for the Taking* (now out of print), he wrote:

> *I invented an impossible God whose demands of me were so high and his opinion of me so low that there was no way to live except under his frown. All day long he nagged me. Why don't you witness more? When will you ever learn self-discipline? Why don't you pray more? Why don't you witness more? How can you allow yourself to indulge in such wicked thoughts? Yield! Confess! Work harder!*
>
> *God was always using his love against me. He'd show me his nail-pierced hands and say, 'Why aren't you a better Christian?' I had a God who down underneath considered me to be less than dirt. Oh, he would make a great show about loving me but I believed the day-to-day love and acceptance I longed for could only be mine if I let him crush everything that was really me. When it came down to it there was scarcely a word or a thought or a feeling or a decision of mine God really liked.*

Can you understand how a man who held such a concept of God as that could have a breakdown? I most certainly can for I have found in my pastoral and counselling experience that underlying many emotional problems is often a faulty concept of God.

I am convinced, again through my experience in the counselling room, that many Christians when they worship do not worship the true God but a caricature of Him.

'How do you see God?' I asked one woman, who was struggling with a deep emotional problem. She thought for a moment and said, 'Judgemental. Distant. Punitive.'

It was no surprise to me when she told me that, although she tried to be a good Christian and read her Bible every day, she found great difficulty in developing a life of intimacy with the Lord. 'I pray to God,' she said, 'but I find it so difficult to worship Him.' Is it any wonder, when she carried in her heart such a false picture of the Almighty?

I urge you, before you go any further, to think through this issue of how you see God, for if you do not see Him as He really is – trustworthy, reliable and good – then those doubts and misgivings will sabotage true worship.

Forgive another reference to C.S. Lewis (there are going to be quite a few in this book!) but in *The Lion, the Witch and the Wardrobe* he tells the story of the children who passed through the wardrobe in their bedroom and found themselves in the magical land of Narnia, which was ruled by the wicked White Witch.

In the house of Mr and Mrs Beaver a reference is made to Aslan, the Lion (a type of Christ in all Lewis's novels) and Susan asks the question, 'Is he safe?' 'Course he isn't safe,' says Mr Beaver. 'But he's good.'[4]

GOD IS GOOD

If we are to understand and engage in the worship of God then we must be held by the conviction that though God may not be safe He most definitely is good.

But what do we mean when we say, 'God is not safe'? In the past, when in my preaching I have referred to the fact that while God is good He is not safe, often people have come up to me at the end of the talk and appeared rather troubled by the remark.

One such person put it to me like this: 'I felt very insecure when you said that God was not safe. What about the text that says, "For he will command his angels concerning you to guard you in all your ways; they will lift you up in their hands, so that you will not strike your foot against a stone" [Psa. 91:11–12]? Are you saying that God's promise in Psalm 91 is not true and that He cannot be depended upon to protect me from harm?'

I pointed out that the psalm quoted is regarded by Jewish rabbis as a messianic psalm and many of today's evangelical scholars see it in this light also. The temptation story confirms this understanding when it describes how our Lord rejected Satan's seductive use of the psalm in Matthew 4:6: 'If you are the Son of God,' he said, 'throw yourself down. For it is written: "He will command his angels concerning you, and they will lift you up in their hands, so that you will not strike your foot against a stone." '

Some Christians try to hold God to promises He never made. As a pastor I have dealt with many believers who have been close to leaving the faith because they considered God did not keep His promises.

When I have asked them to show me the promise from Scripture they believe God did not keep, I find in every case that it was something they had read into Scripture, rather than a specific promise the Almighty has decreed.

It is true that God intervenes at times to protect His children from accidents or sickness but there are no guarantees that He will always guard us from harm.

There have been times in my own life where I have experienced the miraculous intervention of God, delivering me from potentially harmful situations, but there have been times too when I have experienced serious physical harm, such as a car crash in which several of my ribs were broken.

The truth is – and this must be faced – God doesn't always respond to our prayers and wishes in the way we would like. He allows little children to be abused, heals some and doesn't heal others and permits the most awful and terrifying things to happen to some of His people.

Take Joni Eareckson Tada, for example. In her teens Joni dived into shallow water in a lake and broke her neck. In a taped talk to an American audience she said, 'Suddenly God didn't seem so good. Suddenly He seemed uncontrollable, *unsafe*.' (Emphasis mine.)

Unless the issue that God may not be safe but He is good, is established clearly in our minds, understood and accepted, then there can be no advancement in the things of God. No true worship.

Before leaving this issue, let me make clear that though God may not always preserve us from physical harm, He most definitely protects us from spiritual ills. C.H. Spurgeon wrote:

> *It is impossible that any ill should happen to the man who is beloved of the Lord … Ill to him is no ill but only good in a mysterious form. Losses enrich him, sickness is his medicine, reproach his honour, death his gain.*

The poet Rupert Brooke had this same thought in mind (that God keeps our souls safe in the midst of life's most difficult circumstances) when he wrote:

> *Safe shall be my going,*
> *Secretly armed against all death's endeavours.*

Safe where all safety's lost, safe, where men fall.
And if these poor limbs die; safest of all.

SERVICE – ITS PROPER PLACE

As an observer of the Christian scene for most of my life I have noticed that God's people are often more taken up with working for Him than with worshipping Him.

But when we put work first and worship second we get it wrong. The most important aspect and the central focus of the Christian life is not what we can do for Him but what He has done for us. Get that the wrong way round and you will most definitely experience spiritual problems.

Sometimes in the past when I have visited other countries I have been approached by missionaries who tell me that they are about to be invalided home because of overwork. When talking to them I find that, though they have been working for God, they have lost touch with Him in worship. They have been trying to be a spiritual palm or an open flower, but because they did not pursue first and foremost the act of worship then the other things just did not work out.

One of the verses of Scripture I often refer to when talking to groups about this subject is this, 'We love because he first loved us' (1 John 4:19). The central focus of the Christian life is not what we can do for God but what He has done for us. If we reverse that we will end up becoming spiritual casualties.

C.S. Lewis put it well when he said, 'Put first things first and you get second things thrown in. Put second things first and you lose both first and second things.'

I remember an old Welsh miner who used to get up in the testimony meetings in our local church and say, 'I worship God almost every moment I am awake. I live in the presence of worship. I carry a constant thought in my heart that is there when I awake in the morning and still there when I go to sleep at night. That thought is this: it was Jesus my Saviour who wrought this change in me.'

That is what I mean by worship – the awe of God constantly being celebrated in the heart.

Oswald Chambers said, 'The biggest competitor for devotion is service.' Do we put the emphasis on service at the expense of worship? Always remember we are not working to be saved, but working because we are saved.

In one of his books, Os Guinness refers to a man going to the Far East to study different religions. He came back to the United States with this statement: 'When I meet a Buddhist priest, for example, I meet a holy man. When I meet a Christian leader I meet a manager.' He saw how the work orientation, rather than worship, absorbs many of the Church's leaders. How very sad.

Pastors are particularly vulnerable to falling into the activist trap by reason of the fact that in today's world they practise their ministries in an atmosphere of 'compulsive activism'.

People nowadays seem to almost have a nervous breakdown if they miss one section of a revolving door. Almost everyone seems to be rushing here and there and pastors are expected to follow suit. To all overworked pastors our Lord says the same thing as He said to His disciples:

> *'Are you tired? Worn out? Burned out on religion? Come to me. Get away with me and you'll recover your life. I'll show you how to take a real rest. Walk with me and work with me – watch how I do it. Learn the unforced rhythms of grace.'*

Matt. 11:28–29, The Message

'The rhythms of grace.' What a beautiful expression! Those rhythms flow more easily when worship is first and work second.

I appreciate so much what Eugene Peterson says about worship:

Worship is a meeting at the centre so that our lives are centred in God and not lived eccentrically. We worship so that we live in response to and from this centre, the living God. Failure to worship consigns us to a life of spasms and jerks at the mercy of every advertisement, every seduction, every siren. Without worship we live manipulated and manipulating lives. We move in either frightened panic or deluded lethargy as we are, in turn, alarmed by spectres and soothed by placebos. If there is no centre there is no circumference. People who do not worship are swept into a vast restlessness, epidemic in the world with no steady direction and no sustaining purpose.[5]

The worship of God saves us from egoism. It is part of our human nature to identify with any cause we take up. Psychologists warn us that the self-regarding principle is always present and more so when service and not worship is our primary concern.

If service is first and worship second then it will not be long before one finds the self insinuating into the situation. We get caught up in a battle for our own point of view, and tend to live on the praise of others. We can easily abandon projects because of, as one writer put it, 'the stupidity or cupidity of others'.

But we are insulated from all that when worship comes first. God is then our whole reward. Our work is being done for God's sake. If others appear ungrateful for the service that is being given, the ingratitude may hurt but it will not be devastating to the soul. Certainly it can never tempt us to abandon a task which God has set.

My years as a pastor and a counsellor have shown me that such qualities as purity of motive, tenacity of purpose, indifference to reward, self-effacement in service, are all at their highest in those who serve others as a consequence of their worship of God.

As I close this chapter, let me return once more to the image of the carved figures on the walls of Solomon's temple. What do the images of the cherubim, the palm tree and open flower carved on the walls of the house of God in both its inner and outer rooms mean? Those who experience God in worship will find that experience will lead to service for Him, and service brings beauty where ugliness reigns.

We are called by the sacred symbolism of Scripture to be involved in renewing the world and we can only do that when, like the cherubim, we offer the highest worship of which we are capable. And as we respond like the palm tree moved by the wind our lives will bring beauty where ugliness reigns and spread the perfume of the loveliness of Christ in this damp, dark dungeon we call the world.

We are called to be nothing less than worshippers, workers and witnesses to His grace. But worshippers *first*.

Law 2

COUNT YOUR BLESSINGS

Cb

DEVELOP THE ATTITUDE OF GRATITUDE

Thou hast given so much to me ... give me one thing more,
a grateful heart. (George Herbert)

Sir John Templeton is a world-famous financier and philanthropist. His objective in making money, he once said in an interview, was to give most of it away. Year by year he gives away millions of dollars to organisations and charities all over the world. The Templeton Award for Excellence is well known and coveted.

Every morning when Sir John awakes he lies quietly on his bed and thinks of five new ways in which he has been blessed. He says that he finds this simple procedure spiritually enriching and believes that this is one of the chief reasons why so much peace and contentment floods his life.

I wonder how your day begins. Do you pour yourself a cup of coffee, turn on the radio or television to get the latest news report, at the same time exposing yourself to the countless advertisers who tell you what you must do to make yourself happy? If so, then you might be better off adopting Sir John Templeton's approach by lying quietly in your bed after you have awakened and thinking of five new ways you have been blessed.

FOCUS ON YOUR BLESSINGS

As a counsellor, one of the things I have noticed is that people who focus more on the good things that happen to them than the bad are more buoyant, more confident and more positive than those who take things for granted.

It is another law of life, I believe, that the more we dwell on what we have, rather than what we don't have, the more the personality is drawn to health.

Of course, there are people who claim that their lives are so beset with troubles and trials that they have nothing to be thankful for. But, if you cultivate the right perspective, there is something to be thankful for in every situation.

An old Welsh Methodist preacher by the name of Robert Jones was well known for his ability to always find something to be thankful for. One Sunday as he made his way to church he was caught in a tremendous downpour of rain. He arrived at the church just as the service was about to start and, being a stickler for punctuality, refused the appeal of the deacons to change into some dry clothes.

As he entered the pulpit he invited the congregation to bow their heads for the opening prayer. 'We thank Thee, O Lord ...' he began. The congregation, seeing his bedraggled condition, wondered what he would thank the Lord for on this occasion.

Raising his voice he said once again, 'We thank Thee, O Lord ...' Pausing for a few seconds he lifted his voice still more and said, 'We thank Thee, O Lord ... that it isn't always like this!'

I once preached a Sunday sermon in my church in central London on the theme 'A recipe for thanksgiving'. After the service a man came up to me and said that he had nothing to be thankful for. Life had dealt hardly with him, he claimed. He had no job and the unemployment benefit he received did not allow him to enjoy the luxuries of life such as the theatre, meals out in restaurants and so on.

I invited him to join me the following day on my pastoral rounds. Monday was always the day when I tried to pack in as many pastoral visits as possible. We began in court where I had agreed to speak on behalf of a man who had been caught selling drugs, but had since become a Christian.

Before it was my turn to speak we watched a procession of down-and-outs being brought before the magistrates for all kinds of minor offences. Etched on their faces was the pain of emptiness and despair.

I didn't say anything to my companion but I wondered what he thought as he watched this procession of people who were less fortunate than himself.

From there we moved to a hospital to see one of my church members, a woman of thirty years of age who had lost her sight when a gas boiler burst in her home and damaged her eyes.

Not far away from her, in the same ward, also from our church, a woman who had given birth to a still-born baby.

From there we went to an institution for the aged and the poor. Local ministers took services there every Monday and this day it was my turn. About seventy or eighty people sat in a room at midday waiting for the 45-minute service to begin. Many of them were in a pitiable condition.

Some were hard of hearing or quite deaf, some had poor sight or were quite blind, others were hardly lucid and most were unable to find the page in the hymnbook from which we were singing.

When the service was over we slipped into a café on the Strand for a bite to eat and my companion asked me where I was going next. I said I was going to see a couple who were one-time missionaries in the Far East but who had contracted a disease which was so horrific that they could not expose themselves to the public gaze.

'Once a month I visit them, pray with them and give them communion. After that I am due to visit a children's hospital and try to cheer up the eight-year-old daughter of one of my church members – she has a terminal illness.'

He sat quietly for a few moments and then said, 'I don't think I will come with you on the afternoon visits. I have seen enough. Never again will I say I have nothing to be thankful for.'

Having seen so many people less fortunate than himself his perspective had changed.

LOOK FOR THE GOOD

Another thing I have noticed in my work as a Christian counsellor is how so many become preoccupied with the bad things that can happen in life. This is often made worse by the spread of communication which has become so sophisticated in recent decades. As I am sure you have noticed, the world is flooded with bad news, and this is making people depressed at a time when prosperity in the developed countries is greater than ever. Many newspapers interpret everything in bearish terms. And this has a distressing effect. There is only a certain amount of bad news one can take.

Gary Moore, a member of the Board of Advisors for the John Templeton Foundation, tells of interviewing Sir John on the subject of the good and bad encounters he had had with the media over the years. Here's what Sir John had to say:

> *There has always been something in human nature that makes you buy a newspaper that has the most horrible headlines. Because of that, to be successful in the publishing or television business, you have to feed the public these catastrophes or the negative viewpoint. Therefore the public is brainwashed. There are not enough people who are independent enough to do their own analysis and studying and see that, yes, there are problems but for every problem there are at least ten blessings.*[1]

'For every problem there are at least ten blessings!' Is that really so? My experience says it is.

What would happen if we cultivated the attitude of looking for the blessings that crowd into our lives instead of focusing only on the bad things that happen to us? I will tell you. Life would take on a whole different meaning.

Charles Spurgeon, the great London preacher who had such influence in the nineteenth century, said this:

> *It is a delightful and profitable occupation to mark the hand of God in the lives of His ancient saints and to observe his goodness in delivering them, His mercy in pardoning them, and His faithfulness in keeping his covenant with them. But would it not be more interesting and profitable for us to notice the hand of God in our own lives?*

Dr W.E. Sangster, another influential London pastor, now deceased, tells an interesting story in one of his books concerning the business depression that took place in the United States in the last century.[2]

A group of ministers sat together in a room discussing the state of affairs in the nation. One of them said, 'I have got to preach on Thanksgiving Day and I want to say something affirming; but what can I say that is affirming in a period of depression such as this?'

One of the ministers who was present and heard that statement, Professor William Stidger of the School of Theology in Boston, Massachusetts, took those words to heart and for the next few days began to think of the blessings he had received in life and for which he was truly thankful.

As he reflected on his life there came singing into his consciousness the memory of a school teacher who had taught him in kindergarten and of whom he had not heard for many years. Although it was a kindergarten class he still remembered that she had instilled in him a love of verse, something he had been grateful for all his life.

Realising that he had never thanked her for her contribution to his life he sat down and wrote a letter of thanks to the old lady. A few days later he received this reply, written in a feeble scrawl:

My dear Willie,

I cannot tell you how much your note meant to me. I am in my eighties, living alone in a small room, cooking my own meals, lonely and like the last leaf of Autumn, lingering behind. You will be interested to know that I taught in school for fifty years and yours is the first note of appreciation I ever received. It came on a blue-cold morning and it cheered me as nothing has in many years.

The professor wept when he read that note. It prompted him to think of others who had been good to him and he remembered one of his old bishops who had gone out of his way to encourage him at the beginning of his ministry.

The bishop was now in retirement and had recently lost his wife so he wrote him a belated letter of condolence and thanks. This was the reply he got from the aged cleric:

My dear Will

Your letter was so beautiful, so real, that as I sat reading it in my study, tears fell from my eyes; tears of gratitude. Then before I realised what I was doing, I rose from my chair and called her name to show it to her – forgetting for a moment that she was gone. You will never know how much your letter has warmed my spirit. I have been walking about in the glow of it all day long.

I tell you it pleases not only people but God also when we show our appreciation to those who have helped us on the way. The Almighty often sends His special blessings by way of people and I think He likes His agents to be thanked also. We need to be aware that mercies stream to us not only from heaven but from our fellow men as well.

How sad it is when a man or woman demonstrates the opposite of thankfulness – ingratitude or peevishness. An incident in the life of King Hiram illustrates this better than any other section of Scripture I know.

King Solomon, in return for the many favours King Hiram had given him, presented him with the gift of twenty towns which were north of Galilee. But Hiram was not impressed with Solomon's gift. In fact he hated it. Here's the story:

> At the end of twenty years, during which Solomon built these two buildings – the temple of the LORD and the royal palace – King Solomon gave twenty towns in Galilee to Hiram king of Tyre, because Hiram had supplied him with all the cedar and pine and gold he wanted. But when Hiram went from Tyre to see the towns that Solomon had given him, he was not pleased with them. 'What kind of towns are these you have given me, my brother?' he asked. And he called them the Land of Cabul, a name they have to this day.
>
> 1 Kings 9:10–13

Because King Hiram did not like the cities Solomon had given him he called them by the name *Cabul,* a Hebrew word-play, meaning 'as nothing'.

Apparently, in those days, according to Eastern etiquette, anyone who gave a gift expected one in return. King Hiram had given Solomon 120 talents of gold and in return Solomon made him a gift of twenty towns.

But the gift of twenty towns was not what he wanted so he called them by a name that reflected his peevishness – 'Nothing'. Was it not Shakespeare who said, 'Blow, blow thou winter wind, thou art not so unkind as man's ingratitude'?

One wag said there are two kinds of people in the world – those who say there are two kinds of people and those who don't! As far as thanksgiving is concerned, humanity can be divided into two groups: those who take things for granted and those who take things with gratitude. My concern throughout most of the days of my ministry has been to increase the number of those who take things with gratitude.

I came across this the other day, the source of which I have not been able to trace:

Today, upon a bus, I saw a lovely maid with golden hair,
I envied her, she seemed so bright, and wished I were as fair.
When suddenly she rose to leave, I saw her hobble down the aisle;
She had one foot and wore a crutch, but as she passed she smiled.
O God, forgive me when I whine;
I have two feet and the world is mine.

And then I stopped to buy some sweets;
the lad who sold them had such charm.
I talked with him and he said to me, It's nice to talk with folks like you;
You see, he said, I'm blind.
Oh God, forgive me when I whine;
I have two eyes and the world is mine.

Then walking down the street I saw a child with eyes of blue.
He stood and watched the others play

But seemed he knew not what to do.
I stopped for a moment and said:
Why don't you join the others, my dear?
He looked ahead without a word and then I knew –
He could not hear.
O God, forgive me when I whine;
I have two ears and the world is mine.

Someone has said that the most foolish person in the world is that person who focuses on what he or she does not have to the exclusion of what they do have. I agree. If we would spend as much time dwelling on our blessings as we do our difficulties we would be a good deal better off spiritually and psychologically.

How different life is when we learn to develop a trawling eye to look for the good things that happen in our lives.

When I was a boy we used to sing this song in the church I attended:

Count your blessings, name them one by one;
Count your blessings, see what God has done;
Count your blessings, name them one by one;
And it will surprise you what the Lord has done.

One preacher says this is good but impossible advice. You can't count them; your arithmetic is not good enough. There are scores of them which you are not even aware of. But you can think of *some* of them.

CHOOSE TO BE THANKFUL

Do you find it difficult to think of things for which you can be grateful? Then open up your Bible to Psalm 103. Here's how the opening section reads:

> *Praise the* Lord, *O my soul;*
> *all my inmost being, praise his holy name.*
> *Praise the* Lord, *O my soul,*
> *and forget not all his benefits –*
> *who forgives all your sins*
> *and heals all your diseases,*
> *who redeems your life from the pit*
> *and crowns you with love and compassion,*
> *who satisfies your desires with good things*
> *so that your youth is renewed like the eagle's.*

Psa. 103:1–5

The psalmist goes on for another twenty verses and finishes on the same note: 'Praise the Lord, O my soul.' You can't help but feel that as he writes he is experiencing what one writer has called 'the spontaneous overflow of a swelling heart'.

'But I don't always feel like that,' I have heard people say, 'and surely to praise God when you don't feel like it is hypocrisy.'

Let's look at that argument a little more closely. Notice how the psalmist begins: 'Praise the Lord, O my soul.'

See what he is doing? He is charging his soul to praise the Lord. He is saying, in effect, I am going to use my will to stir up my mind to focus on reasons why I should praise the Lord. I may not feel like doing it but I am going to do it anyway!

We can choose to praise God whether we feel like it or not. We don't have to wait until something happens that evokes praise in our heart; we can by an action of our will stir our minds to contemplate the goodness of God, and when we do that, a law of the personality goes into action, namely that what we think about will soon affect the way we feel. I have never found it to fail.

No matter how difficult things are you have a choice to praise Him or not praise Him, to thank Him or not thank Him. It's sad when Christians wait until they feel like praising rather than using their wills to command their minds to focus on reasons for praise.

Stirring his mind to action brings up a number of reasons for the psalmist to praise – eight in fact: divine benefits, forgiveness, healing, redemption, love and compassion, satisfaction and renewal.

He begins, as we said, by charging his soul not to forget God's benefits and soon, as his mind goes to work to identify those benefits, his emotions follow his thoughts like little ducks follow their mother on a pond. And when after twenty-two verses he comes to an end, you feel that it is either his pen or his parchment that have run out and not his stream of praise.

And it all started with a charge to his soul not to forget the Lord's benefits.

How quickly we forget! We forget past mercies and blessings and we are all the poorer because of it. We would be much calmer and more confident in the presence of new troubles if we had remembered vividly the old deliverances; if we had kept them fresh in mind and been able to say, 'The God who delivered me then will not desert me now.'

Remember how John Newton put it in his hymn:

His love in times past forbids me to think
He'll leave me at last in trouble to sink.

One of the reasons I believe we are so fearful in the presence of new dangers is because we forget the good things God has done for us in the past. Many Christians keep what they call a 'Gratitude Journal' and when they need to remind themselves of reasons to praise they open it up, and then praise rises because it must.

Dr Martyn Lloyd-Jones said we would forget the Lord's death if it were not for the commandment to come regularly to His table.

THINK – AND GIVE THANKS

I said earlier that it is a law of life that what we think about affects the way we feel. This is a concept that is well known to psychologists. A whole school of counselling exists, based on this truth, called Rational Emotive Therapy. It says change your thinking and you change your feelings and the next consequence is a change in behaviour.

Remember what Paul told the Philippians:

Finally, brothers, whatever is true, whatever is noble, whatever is right, whatever is pure, whatever is lovely, whatever is admirable – if anything is excellent or praiseworthy – think about such things.

Phil. 4:8

If you want to put this law to the test then clear your mind right now of everything else and begin to focus on all the benefits that God has showered upon you.

Think first of the *common* blessings of life – the blessings so easily overlooked. Food, water, air to breathe, energy to do life's tasks, sight, hearing, reasoning ability, the fruits of the earth.

How prolific is the earth! It requires the sweat of our brow to bring forth some of its fruits but we must never forget that the sweat of our brow without the blessing of God would be of no avail whatsoever. We toil and God adds His blessing. Imagine what life on earth would be like if God withdrew His blessing.

Think also of the love of friends and family. What would your life be like without the love and friendship of others? The eternal God designed it this way. Love and friendship are great blessings; it is sad that so many fail to appreciate them until after they are gone.

If you fell sick is there someone to help? Many people do not have that consolation. This is why God has set the solitary in families so that we can be blessed in this way.

If you suffered bereavement would there be someone to ease your burden and bring solace to your broken heart? I know there are sometimes difficulties among family members, and friends often fall out, but there are positive things, too. Birthdays, anniversaries, the mystery of presents at Christmas, the laughter of children, and so much more. So much more!

Think also of those *special blessings* that come to you, but which are very often forgotten. We refer to them as coincidences but when you look carefully at them in the light of providence they often turn out to be God-incidences. A telephone call at the right moment. A letter that lifts your spirit. An unexpected gift. At first you may not recognise these as coming from God but He is at work in ways beyond our understanding.

Then think again of all of the *spiritual* blessings God has given you. The gift of the holy Scriptures, the Holy Spirit, the companionship of angels and, of course, the Lord Jesus Christ Himself.

The apostle Paul, when writing to the Corinthians on one occasion, broke off from what he was saying and burst out in a paean of praise: 'Thanks be to God for his indescribable gift!' (2 Cor. 9:15). The Living Bible paraphrases this as 'his gift too wonderful for words'. What was so wonderful that it would not go into words? The gift of Jesus Christ! Thanks be to God above everything else, Paul is saying, for Him. What would your life be without Jesus Christ?

One preacher put it like this:

I believe every good thing in my life came from God and – if any doubter wanted to wipe that aside as nothing but an act of faith – I would go farther and say I can actually trace most of them. My deepening conviction that divine love is the only satisfying motive in my life, my life partner, my blissfully happy home, the love of child and friend, the joy of service … they all came as smaller gifts in the hand of the 'unspeakable gift' – from Christ himself.

One of the worst moments for an atheist is when he feels thankful for some special blessing but has no one to thank. You are not in that position. You can trace every good and perfect gift to the Father above.

Now as you contemplate the things I have listed above, do you not feel your heart swelling in gratitude? If you are a Christian I would be surprised if it were not so.

Counting our blessings keeps us oriented to the highest, maintains the concept of reverence in our minds, without which every mortal is deficient. It reminds us who is in charge. So count your blessings and give thanks.

Scripture is replete with texts that encourage us to praise the Lord, be thankful and count our blessings:

Give thanks to the LORD, for he is good; his love endures for ever.

1 Chron. 16:34

Let them give thanks to the LORD for his unfailing love and his wonderful deeds for men.

Psa. 107:31

Give thanks in all circumstances, for this is God's will for you in Christ Jesus.

1 Thess. 5:18

And whatever you do, whether in word or deed, do it all in the name of the Lord Jesus, giving thanks to God the Father through him.

Col. 3:17

But thanks be to God, who always leads us in triumphal procession in Christ and through us spreads everywhere the fragrance of the knowledge of him.

2 Cor. 2:14

In this as in all things Jesus is our example. When He was here on earth He was constantly giving thanks. When He broke the loaves to feed the hungry, He gave thanks. When He healed Lazarus, He gave thanks that the Father had heard Him. When He laid down the Holy Communion, He gave thanks.

Many years ago I lived in the beautiful Towy Valley in a small town called Llandeilo, one of the beauty spots of West Wales.

A friend once came to visit me from Cardiff. I remember thinking as

I prepared to meet him what a beautiful day it was for travelling.

When he arrived at the bus stop I asked him about his journey. All he could talk about was the grime and dirt that spewed out from the steel works at Bridgend.

The road from Cardiff leads through some of the most beautiful country, with scenes of pastoral beauty stretching out on either side, but between Bridgend and Swansea it passes through some rather less salubrious places.

After Swansea it runs into Carmarthenshire, with its rolling hills and its rivers, yet when my friend stepped off the bus his first words to me were, 'You can't believe how glad I am to be here; it was so dismal and depressing in the Bridgend area.'

How long was he in the Bridgend area? Less than fifteen minutes! But he thought only of the gloom. How often do we travel a road that for most part is flooded with sunshine, and yet we dwell only on the shade?

GIVING THANKS IN EVERYTHING

Now of course it must be admitted that it isn't always easy to give thanks. How can you thank God for cancer, for example? As I told you in my Preface, I am fighting a battle with prostate cancer as I write. But I have faith to believe that somewhere at its heart there is a mercy, for I have lived long enough to know there are mercies at the heart of tragedies.

What God allows He also uses. And He never deserts His children, even in the most dire of circumstances, so we can thank Him for that. 'And we know that in all things God works for the good of those who love him,' said the apostle Paul in Romans 8:28. In *all* things!

The great saints of God have always drawn attention to the importance of cultivating a thankful spirit. St Augustine in the fourth century described the Christian as 'hallelujah from head to foot'.

George Herbert, the seventeenth-century Anglican poet, wrote a prayer in one of his poems. I included it at the head of this chapter: 'Thou hast given so much to me ... give me one thing more – a grateful heart.'

G.K. Chesterton said, 'If my children awake on Christmas morning and have somebody to thank for putting candy into their stocking, have I no one to thank for putting two feet into mine?'

W.H. Auden wrote simply: 'Let your last thinks be all thanks.'

Elisabeth Elliot said, 'For one who has made thanksgiving the habit of his life, his morning prayer will be, "Lord, what will you give me today to offer back to you?" '

And it was William Law in the eighteenth century who wrote, 'If anyone would tell you the shortest, surest way to all perfection and happiness, he must tell you to make it a rule to yourself to thank and praise God for everything that happens to you. For it is certain that, whatever seeming calamity happens to you, if you thank and praise God for it you turn it into a blessing.'

The apostle Paul not only told us that in the God-ordained life everything works together for good, but in his letter to the Thessalonians he tells us to rejoice always; and that in everything we ought to give thanks (1 Thess. 5:18).

In everything?

Yes. In everything.

Does that mean we are to thank God for the bad things that happen to us – sickness, accidents, infirmities, and so on? Paul would say, 'Yes!' Everything means everything.

I have heard people say, 'I am not going to give thanks for what that person did to me. It was an evil they planned and it has hurt me more than I can say.'

But if Romans 8:28 is true (and I believe it is) then God only allows into our lives those things that He can turn to good. I take that to mean that if God foresees that a certain situation could arise which He was unable to turn to good then He will not permit it to happen. No matter what happens to you God is committed to working good out of it and because of that it is possible to thank Him for everything that happens to you.

You are not thanking Him for the evil, but you are thanking Him for the good that He is going to bring out of the evil, for the way He is going to redeem the situation and bring something out of it that redounds to His glory.

If you are one of those Christians who finds it difficult to come to grips with this concept, then don't worry. When something happens to you that you feel is evil and you cannot find it in your heart to give God thanks for what has taken place, then start by giving Him thanks for His presence in the situation.

Rejoice that He is a God who is ever-present and who is committed to redeeming the situation.

Then consider this also: He can take the worst thing that has happened to you and turn it into the best thing that has ever happened to you.

Isn't the risen Christ the greatest reminder that even the evil of the cross can be transformed into a new and exalted life? If you start there then I promise you it won't be long before you begin to develop a right response to all the setbacks of life. You will find yourself saying, even in the most difficult of circumstances, 'Thank You, Lord, for letting this happen. I can't wait to see how You are going to turn it to good.'

Of course, you may never see how God turns an evil thing to good. You simply have to trust His Word that it will be so. In some cases the good may not even be seen in this generation. It may be in the next, or even the one after that.

One thing is sure: those who have cultivated an attitude of giving thanks in everything are those who have a deep, settled peace in their soul and a confidence towards the future that nothing will be able to shake.

GOD MEANT IT FOR GOOD

Many years ago I remember hearing Corrie ten Boom speak in a church in London. She and her family lived through the Nazi holocaust and they hid Jewish people in their home who otherwise might have been killed. Eventually she and her older sister Betsy were placed in a Nazi prison camp and it was such a flea-ridden place that she couldn't stand it.

One night, as they were praying and reading the Bible, Betsy said, 'It says here in the first book of Thessalonians that we are to give thanks in everything.'

'Well,' said Corrie, 'I can't give thanks for the fleas.'

Betsy responded, 'Well then, let's give thanks that we are together. Most families have been split up.'

Corrie thought, 'Well, I can do that but I *cannot* thank God for the fleas.'

Much later Corrie found out that one of the reasons why she and her sister were not molested by the guards (as were many of the women) was because their captors were so repulsed by the fleas they would not enter the room.

Corrie said, 'Every day since I discovered that I have given thanks to God for those fleas.'

Some years ago I found myself driving through the little town of Enterprise in Alabama and I remembered the story of how in 1915 a little animal called a boll weevil destroyed much of the cotton in the area and brought about a huge economic crisis. The town depended upon cotton and for a while there was great distress in the community.

Through the calamity, however, the farmers learned to diversify; they learned to plant peanuts, corn and other crops. Eventually the town began to prosper once again so they erected a monument in the centre of the town – to the boll weevil. It was a reminder that through a terrible event good things had happened to the community.

You will remember that there was a moment in the life of the biblical character Joseph who, after having been sold into slavery by his evil brothers, said to them, 'You meant this for evil but God meant it for good.' That was his monument to the power of God to bring good out of apparent evil.

If you have difficulty in identifying things for which to give thanks, then do what a friend of mine does and focus on the fact that whatever blessings have come your way you probably didn't deserve most of them.

If you read the history of the saints you will find them time and time again telling God how undeserving they were of His mercies. That's a sure way of developing the attitude of gratitude.

I saw a cartoon once which pictured a family gathered together for a meal. On one of the walls there was prominently displayed the text, 'In everything give thanks'. The father said to the mother, 'I don't want to complain about leftovers, but haven't we already said grace over this meal three times before?'

He said he didn't want to complain about leftovers, but he did. He wanted to give thanks in all things, but when faced with leftovers he found that a little difficult to do. There is no doubt that the greatest challenge we face as Christians is to give thanks in all things.

I love the story I am about to share and have told it to hundreds of congregations. A minister went to preach in a strange church and prior to the service he was told by one of the deacons that the front pews were always occupied by the inmates of a home for the blind.

The preacher thought that the small group of blind congregants might like to choose a hymn, something with which they were familiar and brought special comfort to their hearts. He asked the deacon if he would find out if there was a hymn they would like sung and while the church official went to enquire, he pondered on their possible choice.

Would it be:

Lead kindly light,
Amid the encircling gloom;
Lead Thou me on?

Or:

Art thou weary?
Art Thou languid?
Art Thou sore distressed?

Or perhaps:

When the weary, seeking rest,
To Thy goodness flee.

When the deacon returned he said, 'They are grateful to you for asking them for their favourite hymn and I am instructed to tell you it is number 92.'

The minister knew number 92 well:

When all thy mercies, O my God,
My rising soul surveys,
Transported with the view, I'm lost
In wonder love and praise.

One of the verses of this hymn reads:

Through all eternity, to Thee
A grateful song I'll raise;
But O, eternity's too short
To utter all Thy praise.

If eternity is too short then begin now. Open your eyes wide to the mercy of God. They couldn't see. But you can. Open your eyes wide to the mercy of God and be thankful.

To sum up, then, it is a law of the soul that the more we focus on what we have rather than what we don't have, the more the soul begins to thrive. So let this be your motto:

Count your blessings.
Let nothing be taken for granted.
Let everything be received with gratitude.
Let everything be passed on with grace.

So *think* – and give thanks!

Law 3

KEEP ON KEEPING ON

Ko

STAYING THE COURSE

In the confrontation between the stream and the rock the stream
always wins – not through strength but through perseverance.
(Thomas Sutcliffe Mort)

Sir Winston Churchill was, without doubt, one of the most extraordinary leaders the twentieth century ever produced. A leader, it has been said, is someone who can see further ahead than those around him.

That was Winston Churchill. He was known also for his ability to stand and face whatever was threatening when others turned back in fear. Even his strongest critics agreed he was a most remarkable man.

Henry Kissinger said of him:

Our age finds it difficult to come to grips with Churchill. The political leaders with whom we are familiar generally aspire to be superstars rather than heroes. The distinction is crucial. Superstars strive for approbation; heroes walk alone. Superstars crave consensus; heroes define them by the judgement of a future they see it as their task to bring about. Superstars seek success in a technique for eliciting support; heroes pursue success as the outgrowth of their inner values. Winston Churchill was a hero.

What was it that enabled him to stand so steadfastly and inspire the British nation (and other nations) to endure great hardships and to fight against all odds?

Perhaps something of the secret is revealed in a story told of him. One day, in his last few years, he was invited to speak at a valedictory meeting in a British university. Due to a mishap with his car he arrived during the last few minutes of the meeting. There was no time for a long speech but he was invited onto the platform and asked to say a few words.

In his gruff manner he looked over the audience of young graduates paused for a few moments and boomed, 'Never give up.' He paused for about thirty seconds and then said, 'Never, never give up.'

Finally, after a much longer pause, he shouted, 'Never, never, *never* give up!'

He then sat down but the audience rose and gave him a standing ovation.

PERSEVERANCE

Later, when writing about the importance of perseverance, Churchill penned these words: 'Never give in, never give in, never, never, never, never – in nothing, great or small, large or petty – never give in except to convictions of honour and good sense.'

The words 'Never give in' are ones Christians should take to heart for, as Peter tells us in his second epistle, perseverance is one of the qualities which enables us to stay the course and live effective and successful Christian lives.

> *For this very reason, make every effort to add to your faith goodness; and to goodness, knowledge; and to knowledge, self-control; and to self-control, perseverance; and to perseverance, godliness; and to godliness, brotherly kindness; and to brotherly kindness, love. For if you possess these qualities in increasing measure, they will keep you from being ineffective and unproductive in your knowledge of our Lord Jesus Christ.*

2 Pet. 1:5–8

Scripture has a good deal to say about this matter of perseverance. It is a law of the soul that those who keep on keeping on and never give up will find their souls fortified for the task.

They will not only find a reward waiting them at the end but they will experience the blessing of God on the way to that reward.

Scripture abounds in texts and passages that remind us that perseverance is required of all the children of God.

The apostle James says:

Blessed is the man who perseveres under trial, because when he has stood the test, he will receive the crown of life that God has promised to those who love him.

James 1:12

The apostle Paul says:

Love does not delight in evil but rejoices with the truth. It always protects, always trusts, always hopes, always perseveres.

1 Cor. 13:6–7

The writer to the Hebrews puts it like this:

Let us fix our eyes on Jesus, the author and perfecter of our faith, who for the joy set before him endured the cross, scorning its shame, and sat down at the right hand of the throne of God.

Heb. 12:2

You need to persevere so that when you have done the will of God, you will receive what he has promised.

Heb. 10:36

The apostle Paul wrote to Timothy:

Therefore I endure everything for the sake of the elect, that they too may obtain the salvation that is in Christ Jesus, with eternal glory.

2 Tim. 2:10

And Jesus said:

'Blessed is the man who does not fall away on account of me.'

Matt. 11:6

The soul will not flourish simply by going to church, singing a few hymns and thinking your Christian duty has been done. Permanent perseverance and persistence, in spite of all obstacles, are what distinguish the strong soul from the weak.

It may be hard being a Christian in the place where you live or work, but God promises to keep us and uphold us in the most arduous of circumstances. Our task is to lay hold of God's strength and keep going no matter what lies ahead.

Listen to this by John Stott:

It is a regular theme of the New Testament authors that the people of God must be steadfast. On the one hand we must resist the intellectual and moral pressure of our contemporary world and refuse to conform to the fashions of the day. We are not to allow ourselves to slip, slither and slide in the mud of relativity or be torn from our moorings and carried away by the flood. On the other hand, and positively we are summoned to persevere in the truth we have received, to cling to it as a secure handhold in the storm, and to stand firm on this foundation.[1]

FOUR REASONS PEOPLE GIVE UP

Why do people fail to be steadfast and persevere? Why do they defect? This is an issue that has exercised me greatly over the years. My research into this subject has revealed that in the main those who fall by the way do so for four reasons.

1. They become discouraged by reason of trials and troubles.

2. They are unable to deal with doubts about the faith.

3. They are overcome by persecution from others.

4. They fall into sin and do not know how to rise again.

1. Trials and trouble

A psychiatrist by the name of Dr Scott Peck begins his book, *The Road Less Travelled*,[2] with this short sentence: 'Life is difficult.' Coming to terms with that fact is essential and important, he says. In fact, understanding that truth and accepting it means that half the battle is accomplished.

Have you noticed that troubles and problems have an uncanny way of coming together? It was Shakespeare who said, 'When sorrows come they come not single spies, but in battalions.' Some days we do well just to survive – to say nothing of excelling. Therefore persevering becomes essential to living, the key that unlocks the door of hope.

Oswald Chambers once made this statement: 'Life is more tragic than orderly. Mystery hangs over this strange law of life that shows troubles come together. Nobody can fully explain why.'

Our Lord said on one occasion, 'In this world you will have trouble. But take heart! I have overcome the world' (John 16:33).

Whenever I read that verse I think of a particular evangelistic crusade I attended some years ago. I sat on the platform along with other ministers and heard the evangelist say, 'Come to Christ and you will have no more problems.'

There were some raised eyebrows on the platform at that moment, I can tell you! Now, if he had said, 'Come to Jesus and you will have someone to help you face every problem', that would have been different. Some problems increase when we become Christians. Sometimes we have to live with friends and families who scorn us because of our commitment to Christ.

Unmerited suffering is a problem for many. Job 5:7 says that 'man is born to trouble as surely as sparks fly upward'. The book itself is in the sacred canon to show us how to deal with unmerited suffering.

Not so long ago a friend of my granddaughter, a young single mother, was bathing her two children when she slipped on the bathroom floor and knocked herself unconscious. When she recovered her two little ones had drowned.

How does one explain that?

The reason why so many are unhappy today is that they fail to understand what human existence is all about. Until we recognise that life is not just something to be enjoyed but rather is a task that each one of us is assigned, we'll never find meaning in our lives and we'll never be truly happy.

I have seen many a person's faith slip away from them when they are beset by difficulties. I read recently about a professor in a Christian university in America who was struck by a large truck and had his leg broken. At his first appearance in the chapel after he recovered he said to the students, 'I no longer believe in a personal God. If there were a personal God He would have whispered to me to beware of the danger of the coming truck and so have saved me from this calamity.' In the crash his faith crashed too.

Many believe that God should spare His children from troubles and calamities. But how ridiculous the world would be if calamities struck the wicked alone and the righteous were always be saved. Its laws would have to be in process of suspension whenever the righteous were involved. Gravity wouldn't pull you over a parapet even though you leaned out too far – provided, of course, you were righteous. If a person was good the law would be suspended; if he were bad it would smite him.

Now that is not to say that sometimes God does not intervene to save His children in particular situations, for He certainly cannot be straight-jacketed in His universe. The laws are His habitual way of running the universe, but to say He cannot overrule them is to make Him less than His modes of action.

When Jesus hung upon the cross, deserted by men and seemingly by God, the crowd cried out, 'He trusts in God. Let God rescue him now if he wants him, for he said, "I am the Son of God" ' (Matt. 27:43).

If it could be proved that the Christian is infallibly spared trials and problems and suffering, the result would be a degradation of Christianity. People would flock to our churches to become Christians as one would take out an insurance policy. It would also be the degradation of the Christian, for he and she would miss the discipline of living in a universe of impartial law.

Listen once again to what Jesus said: 'In this world you will have trouble. But take heart! I have overcome the world.'

Note the words 'Take heart!' Our Lord overcame the trials and difficulties that came His way and because He lives in us, He is able to provide us with the inner strength to persevere and overcome every obstacle that confronts us. All we have to do is provide the willingness; He provides the power.

2. Doubts about the faith

I learned the other day that, sadly, two of the people who were with me in my class in Bible college had left the Christian faith because of doubts that had crept into their minds about Scripture.

There was a time – a dark period in my Christian life – when I had serious doubts about the faith myself. Then I read this: 'Doubt is the other side of faith. No one should worry if there are doubts. They are messages that tell us to turn the coin and we will find the other side to be true.'

That statement brought about a revolution in my soul. The more I pondered it the more I came to see that I should not worry about my doubts but see them as the vestibule through which I must pass in order to enter the temple of truth.

I found great help in what Os Guinness says about doubt:

Doubt is not the same as unbelief. Doubt is a state of mind in suspension between faith and unbelief so that it is neither of them wholly and it is only each partly.[3]

I have met many Christians who think that because doubts enter their minds they have come to the end of faith. Doubt is really faith in two minds. What destroys faith is our unwillingness to confront our doubts and allowing them to harden into unbelief.

Os Guinness points out that the word doubt comes from the Latin *dubitare* which is rooted in an Aryan word meaning 'two'. To believe is to be in one mind about accepting something as true; to disbelieve is to be in one mind about rejecting it. 'To doubt is to waver between the two,' says Guinness, 'to believe and disbelieve at once and so to be in two minds.'

John Newton, the one-time slave-trader who became a Christian and wrote many well-known hymns, wrote to a woman who confessed to having doubts about the faith. This is what he said:

The doubts and fears you speak of are, in a greater or lesser degree, the common experience of all the Lord's people, at least for a time; whilst any unbelief lies in the heart and Satan is permitted to tempt we shall feel these things. In themselves they are groundless and evil; yet the Lord permits and overrules them for good. They tend to make us know more of the plague of our own hearts and feel more sensibly the need of a Saviour and make His rest (when we attain it) doubly sweet and sure. And they likewise qualify us for pitying and comforting others. Fear not, only believe, wait and pray. Expect not all at once. A Christian is not of hasty growth like a mushroom, but rather like the oak, the progress of which is hardly perceptible, but in time, becomes a great deep-rooted tree.[4]

Firstly, we see that doubts are the common experience of most Christians. We must accept the fact that doubts will come and not think them to be a sign that we do not have faith. As the old French proverb puts it, 'Those who know nothing, doubt nothing.'

Secondly, Satan is a tempter. The art of doubting is natural to us in our fallen condition, but Satan often works on our doubts and tempts us to unbelief.

Thirdly, we must continue to believe in the face of our doubts and pray.

Fourthly, it takes time to overcome some doubts and this is why perseverance is a quality that every Christian must cultivate.

Permit me to share with you the way I have dealt with the doubts that have arisen (and sometimes still do) in my Christian life and experience.

Whenever doubt comes I remind myself that to doubt is not to sin. Satan may try to get me to believe that my doubts will put up a barrier between God and me but I know this is not so. I have found that the advice of the apostle James to 'resist the devil, and he will flee from you' (James 4:7) really works. Satan is an imposter. Stand up to him in the name of Jesus and he always backs down.

Next, I pray over the matter, asking the Lord to give me His help in overcoming my doubts and using them as stepping-stones to a deeper faith. George Macdonald said, 'A man can be haunted by doubts and find that he grows thereby because of them.'

'Doubts,' says another writer, 'are the messengers of the Living One to the honest. They are the first knock at our door of things that are not yet, but have to be understood.'

It may not be everyone's experience, but it has certainly been mine, that every deep spiritual assurance I have in my soul has been preceded by varying forms of doubt. Just as a bone becomes stronger after it has been broken and knit together again, so as I have prayed over my doubts I have found myself becoming, as Ernest Hemingway put it, 'strong at the broken places'.

Finally, I bring all my doubts to the judgment bar of Scripture where God has provided for us so many 'infallible proofs'. John Stott points out in one of his books that there is no point in moaning that we seem to suffer from doubts when God has given us the means to increase our faith:

Consequently, faith comes from hearing the message, and the message is heard through the word of Christ.

Rom. 10:17

John Stott adds, 'We have to take time and trouble to hear in order to believe.'

My counselling experience has shown me that those who defect from the Christian Church because of doubts are those who have indulged their doubts and have not laid them against the certainties of the Word of God. As Frances Ridley Havergal put it, 'Doubt indulged soon becomes doubt realised.'

It is vital for Christians to understand that God has condescended to our weakness by giving us the Holy Scriptures, which are stored with powerful truths and concepts able to quench the fiery darts of the devil.

So many Christians complain of spiritual doubt while all the time they do not use the secret weapon which God has put into our hands – His holy and infallible Word.

So when doubts arise, persevere through them by following the principles I have just delineated. Then you will find, as Alfred Lord Tennyson put it:

> *He fought his doubts and gather'd strength*
> *He would not make his judgement blind,*
> *He faced the spectres of the mind*
> *And laid them; thus he came at length*
> *To find a stronger faith his own.*

3. Persecution

It's tough being a Christian in today's world. Time was when people respected Christians even though behind their backs they might ridicule them.

On television Christians are often portrayed as wimps. The modern view it seems is that to be a devout Christian is to be something less than a full man or woman, to be a little silly, to have a vacancy of mind.

People laugh at these caricatures and it would be wrong not to admit that such poor examples exist. But to reason from these few to the whole is as foolish as saying all boys like to wash their necks because a few rare paragons delight to do so.

It must be understood that there is a reproach in the gospel. In Hebrews 13:13 we read: 'Let us, then, go to him outside the camp, bearing the disgrace he bore.' What does it mean, outside the camp? We need to go back to the Old Testament sacrifices for the answer. The instructions of the Lord were that if the whole assembly of the people sinned a young bullock must be sacrificed and when the blood of the bullock had been sprinkled in the holy place the carcass was then carried outside the camp, lest it pollute the place where the people lived.

It was called a sin offering for the whole assembly and a sin offering could not remain within the camp.

Students of Scripture who see in Jesus Christ the consummation of the Old Testament sacrifices point out that when evil men brought about the death of our Lord they took Him outside the walls of the city to a place of crucifixion called Golgotha.

Our Lord was cast out, despised and rejected by men. So the author of the Hebrews says, 'Let's go to him there, outside the camp.'

The epistle to the Hebrews was written to men and women who were undergoing severe persecution for their faith and the author, writing under the inspiration of the Holy Spirit, seeks to encourage them to persevere.

Don't give up meeting together, he says in one place; you can draw strength from one another as you fellowship together. The letter is filled with encouragement and advice on how to persevere. Then he gives them this final piece of advice: 'Let us, then, go to him outside the camp, bearing the disgrace he bore.'

We live in an age that is increasingly hostile to Christians – some countries more than others. There has always been a reproach in the gospel, always a shame at the heart of the cross. You cannot have the friendship of the world and the friendship of Christ. It has to be one or the other. There is a choice to be made and if you are going to be a disciple of Christ then you have to make it.

Many people give up the Christian faith because of that. One young man said to me, 'None of my friends would recognise me; they severed all friendship.' What do we do when that happens? We should exult in it!

Listen again to the word from Hebrews: 'Let us go forth.' Hear the eagerness in the phrase. We are not going to be dragged; we are going to do it willingly. Indeed we run!

We are going to put our shoulders underneath His cross and bear whatever we can by His grace of His reproach. A hymn we used to sing puts it well:

I'm not ashamed to own my Lord
Or to defend His cause
Maintain the honour of His Word,
The glory of His cross.

C.S. Lewis in his *Screwtape Letters*, the advice of a senior devil to a junior devil, says that the routine of adversity, the gradual decay of youthful loves are what wear Christians down. He points out also that suffering is probably not an obstacle to Christians since human beings have been told it is an essential part of redemption. Screwtape rues the man who feels that every trace of God has vanished and asks why he has been forsaken and yet still obeys.

What kept our Lord on the path to the end? We have a clue in the words, 'I delight to do your will, O God.'

I asked a group of senior citizens – all believers – this question: What motivates you to persevere and be steadfast in the Christian life? These were some of the answers I received:

Some said (and I was surprised how many), the fear of going to hell. Others said a sense of duty. One group said, because I want to get to heaven.

Only one person said, 'Because I want to be obedient to the divine will.' Was it not obedience that kept our Lord persevering to the end? The writer to the Hebrews says, 'Here I am – it is written about me in the scroll – I have come to do your will, O God' (Heb. 10:7).

What keeps you in the path of righteousness? Are you kept there by a fear of hell, or can you say with your Lord, 'I delight to do your will, O God'?

How is this delight obtained to keep going on? What is the secret of not just doing one's Christian duty but delighting in it? I think this illustration might help. As a pastor I used to visit the home of an old woman who was being tended by her devoted daughter. I was impressed by the way her daughter cared for her, anticipated all her wants and made her life sweetly bearable despite the prostration of old age.

On one occasion, when I had an opportunity to talk to the younger woman alone, I asked why she did this; after all there were homes available, or the social service could do it. Was it out of a sense of duty, or was she afraid of what her relatives might say?

'No,' she said, 'it is a delight to do it for her. You see, I love my mother. I would do anything for her.'

There was the secret – she loved. And those who love delight to serve.

That is the secret of those who delight to do the will of God. They have come to know God in Jesus and behind the dictates of conscience stands a loving person. To them sin is not just a broken rule; it is a wound in His heart.

Goodness is not merely duty well done; it is a direct and deliberate serving of the Beloved and hence a joyous delight. If you go to a lover of Jesus and say, 'Don't you get bored with going to church, reading the Bible, putting up with all kinds of persecution? Honestly now, aren't there times when you would like to have your fling?' you will get an answer like this: 'You see, I love Jesus, and because I love Him, I delight to do His will.'

Psalm 112:1 says this: 'Praise the LORD. Blessed is the man who fears the LORD, who finds great delight in his commands.'

4. When you fall into sin

How do you deal with yourself when you stumble and crash, when you are so engulfed in shame that you are ready to give up?

Here is the advice I have given to thousands who have found themselves in this situation.

First, don't try to minimise the sin. Many of our problems arise from the fact that we do not see sin in its proper light. Don't just call a sin a mistake or use other euphemisms. It is foolish to call a serious thing by a light name and try to sneak it past your moral guard. Adultery is adultery – not a misdemeanour. Glossing things over by using euphemisms is one of the ways in which we grease the path to waywardness.

And don't be among those who say, 'Everyone sins, so I will too.' Paul answered that false reasoning when he said:

Rather, clothe yourselves with the Lord Jesus Christ, and do not think about how to gratify the desires of the sinful nature.

Rom. 13:14

Secondly, don't persuade yourself that the thing you did was justified by the circumstances. I once asked a woman who had got entangled in an affair how she had got into that situation.

She said, 'My husband was away and I was lonely.' Other people are lonely and don't behave in that way. The loneliness was a factor but the real problem was the lack of firm moral resolve. Admit the sin and don't excuse yourself.

Then go to God, tell Him how sorry you are and ask His forgiveness. Once you have done that, don't brood over the past – He will give you grace to enable you to do that. 'No-one who puts his hand to the plough and looks back is fit for service in the kingdom of God' (Luke 9:62).

STOP PLAYING

A scene fills my memory as I write. I am sitting on a beach in West Wales with my wife and our two sons. In the distance is a farmer who is ploughing his field and one of my sons, after looking at him for a while, tries to copy him by making furrows in the sand.

For my son it was so easy. The man was hard at work, the boy was only playing. Some people are playing at being Christians. But Jesus said that stern and strenuous discipline is needed, and a resolute will.

When Saul of Tarsus was converted he went to live for a few days in a street called 'Straight'. That is the street in which all who are truly converted should live.

Another story I came across in a book written by Os Guinness, *The Call*, illustrates the joy that comes from seeing a work well done. It concerns a woman by the name of Jane Lucretia D'Esterre, who lived in Scotland in the year 1815.

She was then eighteen years old with two small children and was evidently vivacious, talented and beautiful. But she was also orphaned, penniless, alone and recently widowed.

One day she pondered ending her life in the waters of the little river Ecclefechan. Death beckoned her to the stillness of peace. We pick up the story as she gazes into the dark depths of the river:

She looked up and saw a young ploughman setting to work in a field on the other bank of the river. He was about her age but quite oblivious to her and to anything but his work. Meticulous, absorbed, skilled, he displayed such a pride in his work that the newly turned furrows looked as finely executed as the paint strokes on an artist's canvas.

Despite herself Jane Lucretia was fascinated. Slowly she was drawn into the ploughman's pride until admiration turned into wonder and wonder into rebuke. What was she doing collapsing into self-pity? How could she be so wrapped up in herself when two small children were dependent on her?

Rebuked and braced, she got up, returned to Dublin and resumed life – saved from suicide and reinvigorated for life by the sight of work well done.[5]

Who knows that someone might be watching you as you go about your task, some younger Christian perhaps.

RUN THE FULL RACE

The Boston Marathon in the USA is a popular event and attracts some of the best runners in the world. In the spring of 1980 the first woman to cross the finishing line was Rosie Ruiz. Amidst cheering crowds and a blaze of lights she had the coveted laurel placed upon her head, but someone noticed that her legs had lots of loose flesh – cellulite.

An investigation was made and the truth came out: she had entered the race only at the last mile.

How many Christians are like Rosie? They want to get in on the finish but don't want to run the full race! They appear in church on Sundays, but they do not persevere and engage in a personal life with the Lord through the days of the week. They don't go through the tough times, praying through the loneliness and keeping on and staying true during the lonely, anxious hours. Eugene Peterson calls these people 'religiopaths'. Rosie Ruiz was called a sociopath.

> *I don't know about you, but I'm running hard for the finish line. I'm giving it everything I've got. No sloppy living for me! I'm staying alert and in top condition. I'm not going to get caught napping, telling everyone else all about it and then missing out myself.*
>
> 1 Cor. 9:26–27, *The Message*

So never give up.

> *How could we! Even though on the outside it often looks like things are falling apart on us, on the inside, where God is making new life, not a day goes by without his unfolding grace.*
>
> 2 Cor. 4:16, *The Message*

Two frogs fell into a vat of cream. They tried very hard to get out by climbing up the side of the vat but it was too slippery and steep. They could not get a purchase to hop out. Each time they slipped back again.

Finally one frog said to the other, 'We'll never get out of here. I give up.' So down he went and eventually drowned.

The other frog decided to keep trying and kept kicking and kicking hoping he would get some purchase and be able to hop out.

Eventually the constant kicking turned the cream into butter, and so with one final effort the frog leapt out.

If there is one person who comes to my mind whenever I think of the word perseverance it is Jeremiah. He had some pretty hard times to put up with but he never allowed himself to get into a rut.

How did he manage it? I am sure the great man did not resolve to stick it out for twenty-three years, no matter what. Rather, he got up every morning with the sun. The day was God's day, not the people's. He didn't get up to face rejection; he got up to meet with God. He didn't rise to put up with another round of mockery; he rose to be with his Lord.

That is the secret of the persevering pilgrimage – not thinking with dread about the long road ahead but greeting the present moment with obedient delight and with expectant hope.

Another biblical incident which helps us uncover the secret of finding strength in God to continue when your world is in ruins can be found in 1 Samuel chapter 30.

The time is about 1015 BC. The place is Ziglag, a little Philistine town some forty miles south-west of Jerusalem. This is what has happened.

David, fleeing for his life from King Saul, offered his services and those of his 600 men to King Achish, a local Philistine ruler. Achish in return had given the little village of Ziglag to David and his men for their home and the soldiers had brought their families.

David and his men marched with the rest of Achish's troops on an assignment against Israel, but some of Achish's leaders refused to trust David and his men in a battle against their own people and sent them packing.

When David returned to Ziglag he found it in smoking ruins. The Amalekites desert raiders had sacked it, burned it and taken as slaves everyone they had found. Six hundred homes and families were simply gone.

We read in 1 Samuel 30:4, 'So David and his men wept aloud until they had no strength left to weep.'

Then David's men turned on him and blamed him for their troubles. In fact at one moment they were on the point of stoning him (v.6). How could he go on?

He was severely depressed and disconsolate. Had he stopped there it would have been the end of his career and his life. Here comes one of the Bible's great 'buts':

But David found strength in the LORD his God.

FOCUS ON GOD

It doesn't exactly tell us how David went about finding strength in God but the theologian Jim Packer suggests that he would have focused his mind on the Lord and centred his thoughts on the promises that God had made to him.

Packer suggests that the secret of recovering your spiritual footing at a time when everything is falling around you lies in the little word 'think'.

Doubtless David would have focused his mind on God. And that is the secret we must learn, to keep our minds on Him – His greatness, His power and, above all, His ability to bring good out of everything.

No matter what happens, God always gives us strength to cope. 'Strength,' says one Bible teacher, 'is really a synonym for "grace".'
Be assured of this – God will allow nothing to happen to you without providing at the same time a corresponding stream of grace.

So keep on keeping on. Never give up.

If the apostle Paul were writing this chapter I think he might conclude with this:

> *Don't give up. If God has called you to do something then make sure you finish it. Struggle is the chrysalis out of which a new vision of God comes. When pressure comes against you, persevere. God will not let you down. You will find that His strength is more than a match for anything you are called to face.*
>
> *And this doesn't mean you won't feel pressure. What it means is the pressure will never get you down. You will be upheld on the inside. There will be something so strong within that it will support you – no matter what. Oh yes!*

Let the last word be with Emerson who said, 'That which we persist in doing becomes easier – not that the nature of the task has changed, but our ability to do it has increased.'

So never give up.
Never, *never* give up
Never, never, *never* give up!

Law 4

REMEMBER TO FORGET

THE ART OF FORGIVENESS

He who cannot forgive others breaks the bridge over which
he himself must pass. (George Herbert)

It was Christmastime in the home of Dr William Edwin Sangster, one of Britain's foremost preachers, and he was busy sending off the last of his Christmas cards.

One of his guests, who had arrived a few days before to spend Christmas with him and his family, sat with him as he sealed the last few envelopes. He registered his surprise as he caught sight of a certain name and address. 'Surely you are not sending a Christmas card to *him*?' he said.

'Why not?' asked Sangster.

'Surely you remember,' began his guest, 'eighteen months ago ...'

That statement triggered in Sangster's mind the memory of a malicious thing the man had publicly said about him, but he remembered also resolving at the time that, with God's help, he would remember to forget.

Remember to forget. What a strange phrase! Sangster said that he got the phrase from the writings of Immanuel Kant, the famous German philosopher who was born into a Lutheran family in East Prussia on 22 April 1724.

Immanuel Kant never married and lived for years with his trusted manservant Lampe. Then one day he discovered that Lampe had been systematically robbing him and so he dismissed him. Though he missed the services of his 'trusted' servant and often wondered whether he had been right to dismiss him, he eventually came to the conclusion that to get rid of him was the right action.

In his *Journal* there is a pathetic line that reads, 'Remember to forget Lampe.'

How can one remember to forget? Surely the statement is a contradiction in terms. One cannot forget at will. Before I attempt to explain what I mean by remembering to forget permit me for a few moments to address this intriguing subject of memory.

Sometimes we come across people who have an amazing ability for recalling a face, a fact, a name, whenever they want it. We envy such people and wish that we could be like them.

What a precious possession is a good memory. Every week thousands of people respond to the advertisements found in certain magazines offering systems of mind and memory training.

I talked some years ago to one of the directors of a company which offered all kinds of home courses and he told me that out of all the courses the company offered the one dealing with memory training had by far the greatest number of enrollees.

POWER TO FORGET

Precious though a good memory is, the power to forget is equally precious. Henri Gergson, the French philosopher, said, 'It is the function of the brain to enable us not only to remember but also to forget.'

Much of the time I have spent in helping people with their problems over the years has been focused on helping people forget. This is because so often when I have encouraged people to let go of the past with all its hurts and painful memories and to forgive those who have hurt them, they have responded by saying, 'I can forgive but I can't forget.' They forgive but they don't want the other person to forget they have forgiven.

One writer claims that the biggest cause of relationship problems is not things forgotten that should have been remembered, but the things remembered that should have been forgotten. A bad memory can cause huge problems but a bad 'forgettery' even more.

Some of you, I imagine, will smile and say, 'I don't need any instruction in that as I have a pretty good forgettery already. I can forget my spouse's birthday, the day I was married, an appointment I should keep, a promise made to my children,' and so on.

But, I wonder, are you as good at forgetting as you think? It's sad when you keep forgetting things like a close family member's birthday or the date of an important appointment, but at the same time are you remembering something you ought to forget?

Modern-day psychologists believe that apart from an injury to the brain we never really forget anything. Every one of our thoughts and deeds are indelibly imprinted on our memories, they say, and though these things may be beyond the reach of recollection they remain intact in our memory banks.

Operations on the brain while a person is awake have shown that memories long forgotten can be revived. They are just buried in the subconscious, that's all. They may be difficult to recall but when parts of the brain are triggered by electrodes they can be brought back into consciousness.

I have counselled a number of people in my time who have suffered a psychological breakdown when some horrible repressed memory of the past breaks through the defensive fabric of repression causing severe mental and emotional pain.

It may be academic but I think the social scientists have a point: we do not really forget anything, our memories are simply beyond the reach of recall.

Dr Earl Radmacher, a physician and a Christian, says:

I have heard some persons complain that their brain is too tired to get involved in a programme of Scripture memorisation. I have news for them – the body can get tired but the brain never does. The brain is capable of an incredible amount of work and retains everything it takes in. You never really forget anything; you just don't recall it. Everything is on permanent file in your brain.

So if, as Dr Rachmacher says, we never really forget anything, in what sense can we understand the term 'remember to forget'? My Encarta World Dictionary says that the word 'forget' can be used in several different senses:

- *to be unable to recall something;*
- *to fail to give due attention to something;*
- *to stop thinking about an issue.*

The last definition – to stop thinking about an issue – is what I have in mind when I encourage you to remember to forget.

STOP THINKING ABOUT IT

Charles Swindoll says that forgetting in a biblical sense means –

Refusing to keep score (1 Cor. 13:5)
Being bigger than any offence (Psa. 119:165)
Harbouring no judgmental attitudes (Matt. 7:1–5).

It is another law of life, I believe, that spiritual health and success depend on our ability to forget the hurts and injuries that others have given us – not to have them erased from memory, but to deal with them in such a way that we are not emotionally overwhelmed by them.

Failure to observe this law can result in tragic consequences.

Almost every one of us has had things happen in our lives – unpleasant things – which to recall might do us harm; but I believe it is possible that God can help us forget those things, or to remember only as much of them as will be for our own good.

One cannot of course forget the facts; it is the bitterness and the emotional overwhelming from which deliverance may be found.

How many marriages have been shipwrecked because one or both of the partners determined not to forget? And how many churches split over little issues that ought to be forgotten, instead of being the cause of one group going off in a different direction, fractured, splintered and a monument to failure.

My experience is that when we decide that we will not keep score of all the wrongs committed against us, and when we determine to put away our 'hate lists', then God puts at our disposal His divine power to live a life free of bitterness and resentment. He enables us truly to forget.

GOD MAKES US FORGET

A section of Scripture that has often fascinated me in this connection is the story of Joseph, recorded for us in the book of Genesis. I've mentioned it before but now I want to come back to it in greater detail.

Flung into a pit then sold as a slave by his own brothers, lied about by a lascivious woman, thrust into prison and then, after solving the perplexities of Pharaoh's mind, Joseph moves almost in one stride from prisoner to prime minister, with an authority second only to the throne.

If anyone had a reason to keep score it was Joseph. Later, however, when he began to enjoy the blessings of married life, he had a son born to him whom he called 'Manasseh'. The meaning of that name is, 'God has made me to forget'.

Looking into the face of his firstborn son, Joseph realises with deep gratitude, perhaps for the first time, that the sharp edge had come off the bitter memories of the past. God had *made* him to forget.

The birth of a child, especially the firstborn, is for most people a deeply moving experience. One feels mixed emotions – joy and wonder at becoming a mother or father and a certain amount of anxiety as one contemplates the responsibility of nurturing a new life. Perhaps it was the emotion of that moment that caused Joseph to look deep into his soul.

And as he looked he realised that a merciful providence had been at work in his heart. The past had largely been forgotten. He could find no bitterness or sadness in his soul. 'This is what I will name my first child,' he said to himself: ' "God has made me to forget". '

This conclusion of Joseph – that God had *made* him to forget – is often explained by commentators as the result of the natural process of forgetting.

And what a blessing that is!

Everyone is familiar with it. Time heals as we say, and it is quite astonishing how, after a while, the mind stuffs the unpleasant things of life into the hole of oblivion.

Take bereavement, for example – something which all of us in one form or another will have experienced. Do you remember the floodtide of feeling that swept through you when you first lost a loved one? If it was a sudden death then no doubt you felt stunned. If you had time to prepare for it you found at the last that you hadn't prepared at all.

Assuming the bereavement happened years ago, are you able to recall your feelings at that time? For you the sun went out, the world turned grey and perhaps you wished that it was you who had died. Remember? But what is it like now? Mercifully the cutting acuteness of the feelings has passed. Time has healed – to a degree anyway. The feelings of sadness and loss never really go away but time certainly helps. The edge has come off your sorrow. There is still a scar there but, thank God, it is no longer an open wound.

But is this natural process what Joseph was referring to when he said God had made him to forget? I don't think so. There is some truth in it, of course, but the natural process of forgetting cannot deal with all the unpleasant experiences of life. In Joseph's experience, I believe, there was at work not only the natural process of forgetting but a supernatural process also.

In addition to the blessing of natural forgetfulness there is, as Joseph and Sangster found, an ability given by God whereby He helps us deal with the hurts and injuries of the past in a way that *makes* us forget. Unpleasant events of the past no longer rankle in the soul.

FORGIVE AND FORGET

Another passage of Scripture that has come to mean a lot to me personally as I have dealt with past hurts and injuries in my own life (especially in my youth) is this:

> 'Do not be afraid; you will not suffer shame.
>   Do not fear disgrace; you will not be humiliated.
> You will forget the shame of your youth
>   and remember no more the reproach of your widowhood.
> For your Maker is your husband –
>   the Lord Almighty is his name –
> the Holy One of Israel is your Redeemer;
>   he is called the God of all the earth.'

Isa. 54:4–5

The famous psychoanalyst, Freud, said that 'the mind will return again and again to that which gives it pain'. But it need not do so when the things that cause it pain have been replaced by God's peace.

Are you having difficulty in this area of remembering to forget? Have you been deeply sinned against? Has somebody slandered or libelled you or done you a terrible injury? Are you nursing in your heart the hope of revenge?

Then I come to you in God's name and plead with you to deal with it in the way we are commanded to do in Scripture. For your own sake and God's sake make up your mind that you are going to deal with it this very day. However justified your resentment against another person, to harbour that resentment is to poison yourself. Be rid of that poison in God's name.

'Every Christian,' someone has said, 'should be three things: a giver, a forgiver and a forgetter.'

I will talk about being a giver in a later chapter but for now let me help you with the matter of being a forgiver and a forgetter.

If you want God to help you forget then you must first be willing to forgive. You provide the willingness and God will do the rest.

It's not easy to forgive but here you can claim the special help of God. C.S. Lewis said, 'Forgiveness is a wonderful idea until we have someone to forgive.'

There comes to mind, as I write, a counselling session in which a woman said to me, 'That person has hurt me so much that I will not forgive.'

At an appropriate moment (and it is always wise when counselling to understand and empathise with a person's pain before confronting them with the truth of God's Word) I said, 'I understand your hurt and the pain this has caused you and my heart bleeds for you after all the struggles you have gone through, but you have no option in the matter.'

I continued, 'It is a divine law that all hurts and injuries that have been done to you must be dealt with in an act of forgiveness. To hold on to unforgiveness is a violation of that divine law. You *must* forgive.'

'I have never heard anyone say I *must* forgive,' she replied. 'I know it is advisable but surely God understands the difficulties we have in forgiving those who have hurt us.'

I read her these words from the Living Bible paraphrase of Colossians 3:13:

> *Be gentle and ready to forgive; never hold grudges. Remember, the Lord forgave you, so you must forgive others.*

You *must*!

She was silent for a few moments after that but eventually she responded, 'Then God's standards are unbelievably high – higher than I can reach.'

I replied, 'Not only does God lift His standards to almost unbelievable heights but He also provides the power by which we can reach them.'

That led to an interesting discussion, but she was not ready to bring her willingness in line with God's commands until I read her this scripture from Matthew 6:15:

> *'But if you do not forgive men their sins, your Father will not forgive your sins.'*

As prayerfully I watched her struggle to bring her will in line with God's will, I saw what I have seen a thousand times in counselling, that when we set our will in God's direction He is there at our side helping us do what naturally we find difficult to do, that is, forgive.

It was a wonderful moment when she knelt with me in prayer and said, 'Father, You have forgiven me so much and released me from so much guilt and because of that I now forgive … who has hurt me so deeply. I cannot do it in my own strength so I do it in Yours.'

The fact that God has forgiven us is one of the most powerful inducements to forgiveness we can ever consider.

… AS YOU HAVE BEEN FORGIVEN

When people say to me, 'My problem is I can't forgive.' I say, 'No, that is not your problem. Your problem is you don't know how much you have been forgiven.'

A biblical passage brings this point out forcibly. I quote again from *The Message* by Eugene Peterson:

> At that point Peter got up the nerve to ask, 'Master, how many times do I forgive a brother or sister who hurts me? Seven?'
>
> Jesus replied, 'Seven! Hardly! Try seventy times seven.
>
> 'The kingdom of God is like a king who decided to square accounts with his servants. As he got under way, one servant was brought before him who had run up a debt of a hundred thousand dollars. He couldn't pay up so the king ordered the man, along with his wife, children, and goods, to be auctioned off at the slave market.
>
> 'The poor wretch threw himself at the king's feet and begged, "Give me a chance and I'll pay it all back." Touched by his plea, the king let him off, erasing the debt.
>
> 'The servant was no sooner out of the room when he came upon one of his fellow servants who owed him ten dollars. He seized him by the throat and demanded "Pay up. Now!"

'The poor wretch threw himself down and begged, "Give me a chance and I'll pay it all back." But he wouldn't do it. He had him arrested and put in jail until the debt was paid. When the other servants saw this going on, they were outraged and brought a detailed report to the king.

'The king summoned the man and said, "You evil servant! I forgave your entire debt when you begged me for mercy. Shouldn't you be compelled to be merciful to your fellow servant who asked for mercy?" The king was furious and put the screws to the man until he paid back his entire debt. And that's exactly what my Father in heaven is going to do to each one of you who doesn't forgive unconditionally anyone who asks for mercy.'

Matt. 18:21–35

HOW OFTEN?

Consider with me some of the fascinating insights Jesus packs into this story. First, Peter's question:

At that point Peter got up the nerve to ask, 'Master, how many times do I forgive a brother or sister who hurts me? Seven?'

Some commentators say it was a Jewish custom that if someone were to ask forgiveness three times then it had to be given. Others say the custom was that a person could forgive an offence once, twice and three times but if an offence was committed against them for the fourth time then no forgiveness need be given.

It is thought by one commentator that Peter was trying to be magnanimous and more than doubled the number of the prevailing custom.

When Jesus replied, 'Seven! Hardly! Try seventy times seven,' He was not meaning to convey that forgiveness should only be given 490 times. He is suggesting an infinite number of times.

My old pastor and mentor David Thomas used to say about this verse that by the time someone had forgiven 490 times he or she would be so into the habit of it they would keep going for ever. That might well have been the thought in Jesus' mind when He made that statement.

How it must have staggered the disciples to hear the Master expound this truth. Perhaps it was their surprise and astonishment that prompted Him to go into greater detail.

The story Jesus tells is of a servant who owed a king a massive debt of money. It's an amazing sum – one hundred thousand dollars (in *The Message* paraphrase). Some translations put it at ten million dollars! Historians point out that the annual taxes in Judea and Samaria did not come to anywhere near that amount.

Jesus' hearers would have been intrigued by such a sum. It would have got their interest right away. How could a servant be in debt for so much?

Jesus, in telling this story, appeals to their curiosity. He did this all the time; His stories compelled curiosity. Curiosity kills that part of us that lives with self-righteousness. The more curious you are the harder it becomes to maintain self-righteousness.

What is the essence of self-righteousness? Isn't it 'I know'? I know the answer to that. I know how to run my life, how to be a complete person.

The core of all good stories is tension. If there is no tension there will be boredom. Without intrigue you will not stay with the story. You can be sure when Jesus said that there was a servant who owed his master such a fantastic sum, He had their interest.

Clearly Jesus is using hyperbole here – an exaggerated sum for the sake of emphasis. The king, says Jesus, forgave him the debt. Just think of it – a massive debt cancelled in a single moment. It is, of course, intended to show the idea of infinite forgiveness, a beautiful reminder of God's forgiveness to sinners.

But look what happens next. The same servant who had been forgiven such a massive sum meets a fellow servant who owes him a mere pittance – ten dollars – and assaults him. 'He seized him by the throat and demanded, "Pay up. Now!" '

The man was unable to pay so he had him arrested and put in jail until he paid back all he owed.

Some of the king's other servants when they heard about this carried the message back to the king, who was furious. He summoned the man into his presence:

'You evil servant! I forgave your entire debt when you begged me for mercy. Shouldn't you be compelled to be merciful to your fellow servant who asked for mercy?'

The point Jesus is making here is that since we have received such matchless mercy from God we should pass that mercy on to others. The compassion God shows to us, as illustrated by the king in the story, is the kind of compassion we ought to give to those who may have injured us.

Many have wondered why a servant who owed so much could act in such a way towards someone who owed him so little. I have often thought to myself that perhaps the point Jesus wanted to make was that the servant who had been forgiven such a massive debt never really allowed the magnanimity of that act to reach his heart. He knew it intellectually but had never allowed the wonder and joy of it to reach deep inside his soul.

The longest journey in the world, it has been said, is the eighteen inches between the head and the heart.

Whether or not this is what the Lord had in mind my experience shows that many Christians (perhaps far more than we may think) do not have a sense of *realised* forgiveness. They have been forgiven but they have never been overwhelmed by it.

'I'M FORGIVEN!'

One of the things that staggered me when I first became a Christian in my mid teens was the fact that God had forgiven all my sin. I just could not get over it. I thought it was fantastic that all the sins of my youth (and they were many) were all blotted out. It just blew my mind that God had forgiven me.

In the informal mid-week church services, whenever the pastor would ask if someone had a hymn they would like to choose, I would ask that we sing the hymn that contained these words:

My sin – oh the bliss of the glorious thought –
My sin – not in part but the whole,
Is nailed to the cross and I bear it no more.
Praise the Lord, praise the Lord, O my soul!

Then when the pastor would ask if someone had a passage of Scripture they would like to read I would leap to my feet and read this:

Praise the Lord, O my soul;
  all my inmost being, praise his holy name.
Praise the Lord, O my soul,
  and forget not all his benefits –

who forgives all your sins

  and heals all your diseases,

who redeems your life from the pit

  and crowns you with love and compassion,

who satisfies your desires with good things

  so that your youth is renewed like the eagle's ...

he does not treat us as our sins deserve

  or repay us according to our iniquities.

For as high as the heavens are above the earth,

  so great is his love for those who fear him;

as far as the east is from the west,

  so far has he removed our transgressions from us.

Psa. 103:1–5,10–12

It was customary in our church during the mid-week services for the pastor to invite people to give a personal testimony to Jesus Christ. Whenever this invitation was given I was usually the first on my feet to say just two words: 'I'm forgiven,' then sit down.

After a while my pastor came to me and tactfully said, 'It's wonderful to hear what God's forgiveness has meant to you, but do you think you could just say a little more after you have said "I'm forgiven"? I think it would be helpful to you and everybody to hear a little more about your feelings on this issue.'

The wonder of the fact that I have been forgiven has never left me. The tears are flowing down my face now as I write. To be forgiven by God and to be reconciled to Him through His Son Jesus Christ is the most glorious thing that can happen to anyone.

I am convinced that the more we realise what it means to be forgiven the less difficult it will be to pass on forgiveness to others. That is why whenever anyone says to me, 'I have a real problem in forgiving people,' I say, 'I wonder if your real problem is the fact that you don't realise how much you have been forgiven.'

THE CONSEQUENCES OF NOT FORGIVING

Finally we come to what we might call our Lord's punch line to this fascinating story. I have not come across anything in the Word of God as challenging and as intriguing as this:

> 'The king was furious and put the screws to the man until he paid back his entire debt. And that's exactly what my Father in heaven is going to do to each one of you who doesn't forgive unconditionally anyone who asks for mercy.'

The New King James version translates it in this way:

> 'And his master was angry, and delivered him to the torturers until he should pay all that was due to him. So my heavenly Father also will do to you if each of you, from his heart, does not forgive his brother his trespasses.'

To me these are some of the most incredible words in the whole of Scripture. I used to think they meant that if we do not forgive in the same way we have been forgiven then in the next life we will find ourselves in hell. But after much reflection I don't think that was what Jesus was saying.

He is making the point, I believe, that unless we demonstrate forgiveness to others in the same way that we have received it ourselves, then we open ourselves to a terrible toll being taken on our personalities. We will find ourselves incarcerated, shut off from the joys of life, condemned to an inner disruption, which is a torturous experience.

The sin of unforgiveness (for that is what it is – sin) is not held in safe keeping to be let loose upon us in the next world; it takes its terrible toll upon us *now*.

I appreciated the way Ray Steadman put it in a sermon preached at the Bible Peninsular Church, Palo Alto, California many years ago:

> *This is a mysteriously expressive phrase to describe what happens to us when we do not forgive another. It is an accurate description of gnawing resentment and bitterness, the awful gall of hate or envy. It is a terrible feeling. We cannot get away from it. We feel strongly this separation from another and every time we think of them we feel within the acid of resentment and hate eating away at our peace and calmness. This is the torturing our Lord says will take place.*

Who has not experienced such feelings? It happens whenever we decide not to forgive and is a consequence that cannot be avoided.

I have talked to many Christians over the years who have been 'handed over to the torturers' because they would not forgive. Their zest for life was eroded, their creativity shrivelled up, their ability to withstand stress reduced – all because they would not forgive.

Our churches are filled with Christians who know intellectually that they have been forgiven but who lack a realised sense of forgiveness in their heart. It's in their heads, but the amazement and sheer wonder has never reached their hearts.

An unrealised sense of forgiveness underlies, in my opinion, many of the struggles we have when it comes to the forgiveness of others.

In a page of *Every Day with Jesus*, the bimonthly devotional notes I write, I referred on one occasion to the story of the unforgiving servant and mentioned, in just the briefest way, that when we do not carry within our hearts a deep sense of realised forgiveness then a heaviness remains in the personality which can produce not only spiritual problems but psychosomatic symptoms also.

Some time later I received this letter from a medical doctor who had been deeply affected by what I had written:

> As I read your words I realised that I had been living for years with an unrealised sense of forgiveness. Oh I understood it intellectually but the message had never really reached my heart. And because of this I was striving unconsciously to pay back the debt until the muscles of my soul screamed out in pain. The torturers were not long in coming and soon the result of my striving was an allergic sickness that incapacitated me. I got down on my knees after reading your words and asked the Holy Spirit to help me comprehend the wonder of the fact that I had been forgiven, that my debt had been fully paid on Calvary. He did that in a wonderful way.
>
> Now praise God all sense of indebtedness has gone. No longer am I trying to exact payment from myself. No longer need I be driven by a hidden debt that seemed to overwhelm me. I began to realise for the first time in all its depth the meaning of the phrase 'He did it for me'. There is no more debt to drive me in exacting payment from myself. No more debt which goads me to judge others and strive. I'm free. My life is gently being turned around. And in the last few days I have realised my allergic sickness has gone.

The consequence of not forgiving is deeply serious. I can't tell you the number of people I have met in my time who bore all the marks of having been handed over to the torturers; they had become old before their time, wizened, dried up.

Believe me, it's not worth the misery. We are to forgive as we have been forgiven. Nothing is clearer than that in Scripture. Paul wrote to the Ephesians:

> *Be kind and compassionate to one another, forgiving each other, just as in Christ God forgave you.*

Eph. 4:32

And when writing to the church in Colossae he said:

> *Bear with each other and forgive whatever grievances you may have against one another. Forgive as the Lord forgave you.*

Col. 3:13

HOW DO I FORGIVE?

I believe there are three things necessary in order to forgive and forget.

First, *focus on how much you have been forgiven*. Think how extensive God's mercy has been in your life. You may think you have committed only little sins but, as someone has put it, there are no little sins, just as there is no little God to sin against.

Nothing anyone has ever done towards you is as offensive as what you have done to God over the years by ignoring His claim upon your soul and refusing Him admittance into your life. Yet now He has forgiven you, washed all your sins in the blood of His Son, and written your name in the Lamb's book of life.

Take your time over this. Reflect on that fact that you have been forgiven until its truth penetrates deep into your soul.

The poet William Wordsworth wrote:

My heart leaps up when I behold
A rainbow in the sky.

If a poet can get excited about a rainbow in the sky then surely a Christian ought to get excited about a rainbow in the soul – a rainbow that signifies the storm is over and peace is in the heart.

There is a story told of Thomas Chalmers, a great preacher of yesteryear, who one day when preparing a sermon on Paul's words in Galatians 2:20: 'the Son of God, who loved me and gave himself for me', was so struck by Paul's use of the word 'me' that he began to apply it to himself.

He walked over to a mirror and pointing to himself said over and over again, 'Me. Me. It was for *me* he died.' Such was the weight of meaning the words had for him that he ran out into the street and accosted the first passer by with the words, 'It was for me, for me, he died.'

Later, when telling that story to his congregation, many were moved to tears as they realised afresh that while salvation is for all, its impact is limited unless there is the realisation that he did it for 'me'.

Try personalising those words of Paul and apply them to your life. Ponder the depth of God's mercy towards *you*. Reflect on the great debt which you owed Him but which through His wondrous mercy has been cancelled.

The more you can envision the sweep of God's forgiveness towards you, the more you will be able to extend the sweep of your forgiveness to others.

Secondly, *deal honestly with any lingering resentments that may be in your soul.* This is always a challenging moment. No doubt some of you reading these lines will have gone through deep hurts and even deep horror. As you think now of that person who hurt you, abused you, slandered or libelled you, tortured you, rejected you, release the poison of bitterness in Jesus' name. Let it gush out before God and tell Him that you want to be free.

Be prepared to go all the way with God on this. Don't settle for half forgiveness and say, 'I'll forgive but I will never forget.' Limited forgiveness is no forgiveness at all.

Amy Carmichael has something helpful to say about this:

> If I say, 'Yes, I'll forgive but I cannot forget', as though the God, who twice a day washes all the sands on all the shores of all the world, could not wash away such memories from my mind, then I know nothing of Calvary love.[1]

If you find yourself pulling back over this matter of forgiving then it is probably because the wonder of the fact of how much you have been forgiven is still in your head and has not reached your heart. Go back over the first point once again and focus on how much you have been forgiven.

Think also about the consequences of not forgiving and being handed over to the torturers. Unforgiveness is not worth the misery.

And if you think that God is harsh in putting before you this alternative – forgive, or else – then realise that He has your best interests at heart. Your soul was never made to carry the poison of bitterness and resentment. Those are toxins in your personality. You will never rise to be the person God wants you to be when bitterness and resentment is allowed to fester in your soul.

Thirdly, *ask God to help you forget.* If you accept the responsibility to forgive then God will accept the responsibility to help you forget. You can bank on it. You do the possible, God will do the impossible. It's as simple as that.

If you think that all this is too difficult for ordinary human beings to put into effect then may I remind you of the story with which I began this chapter.

When Dr Sangster's guest said, 'Surely you are not going to send a card to him?' that statement triggered in his memory the malicious thing that the person had said about him. But he remembered also resolving with God's help to 'remember to forget'. Mercifully he had forgotten. God had '*made* him to forget'.

He posted the card.

Law 5

GIVE YOURSELF
TO OTHERS

Gy

IMPROVE YOUR SERVE

Arthur Gordon, an American writer, in an article called 'The Turn of the Tide' tells of a time when his enthusiasm for writing waned and no matter how hard he tried his writings brought little or no rewards.

Day by day the situation grew worse. He decided to get help from a physician who, after observing that there was nothing wrong with him physically, gave him this advice:

> *Follow these instructions for one day. Tomorrow, find a place where you were happiest as a child; go to that place but take no food with you. You are not to talk to anyone, read or write or listen to a radio. Here are four prescriptions. You are to open one at nine, the other at twelve, the third one at three and the last one at six.*

The next morning Gordon found a suitable spot on a lonely beach where he used to go as a child, and precisely at nine, as ordered, he opened the first prescription. It read, 'Listen carefully.' At first he was puzzled but soon got the point.

He began to listen to the sound of the sea and to the birds and, as he listened, he began to think of lessons that the sea had taught him as a child – patience, respect for nature, the interdependence of things and so on. The more he listened the more peaceful he felt.

At noon he opened the second prescription and read, 'Try reaching back.' What does this mean? he thought to himself. Reaching back to what?

The first obvious direction to go in his thinking was back to his childhood and as he thought about the early days of his life and the many moments of joy and happiness, he felt an even deeper peace steal into his soul.

At three he opened the third prescription. It read, 'Examine your motives.' The other two had been fairly easy; this one proved difficult. He found himself getting defensive and, as he thought about some of his motives such as success, recognition, security and so on, he found ways of justifying every one of them.

The more he pondered his motives, however, the more he felt that they were not good enough, they were too self-centred and that maybe this was the root cause of his problems.

He concluded:

I saw that if one's motives are wrong nothing can be made right. It makes no difference whether you are a postman, a hairdresser, an insurance salesman, a housewife – whatever. As long as you feel you are serving others you do the job well.

When you are concerned only with helping yourself, you do it less well – a law as inexorable as gravity.[1]

When six o'clock came he opened the final prescription which read, 'Now write out every one of your worries.' He knelt on the sand and with a piece of broken shell wrote out several of his worries, then stood up, turned and walked away. He didn't look back and as he walked he pondered the fact that soon the tide would come in and wash all his worries away.

Arthur Gordon had at that moment what might be described as a paradigm shift – a completely new perspective on life that came with the realisation that life is not about serving yourself but serving others; 'a law,' he says, which is 'as inexorable as gravity'.

The truth is if you are a Christian you have to serve somebody. Your family, friends, neighbours – *somebody*. If you don't share of yourself in some way or another then you demean yourself. Something within shrivels up and your zest for life will diminish.

TIME FOR A CHANGE

Charles Swindoll once wrote a valuable book entitled *Improving Your Serve*. He tells a story of when his book was published. Someone went into a bookshop and asked for it and they were referred to the tennis section! Well. It's not about tennis that we are talking, but about serving others. Flesh-and-blood human beings who can sometimes be difficult, perverse or occasionally downright obnoxious.

The term 'paradigm shift' I understand was coined by Thomas S. Kuhn, a Harvard professor, and appears in his book *The Structure of Scientific Revolutions*.[2]

In that highly-acclaimed volume Kuhn shows how every scientific success required a break with old paradigms, old ways of thinking. Copernicus, he says, created a paradigm shift when he claimed that the old theory of Ptolemy that the earth was the centre of the universe was untrue.

The truth is, said Copernicus, the sun is the centre of the universe. Suddenly, everything looked different. Later Newton came along with his model of the universe and thinking on this subject changed again.

And later still, Einstein, with his relativity paradigm, produced yet another shift.

Who will come along next, I wonder?

Our paradigms – the frameworks we use for thinking about issues – are the sources of our attitudes, our behaviour and the way we relate to others.

SPIRITUAL REVOLUTION

Let me tell you about a paradigm shift which took place in my own life many years ago – a shift which brought about a great spiritual revolution for me.

It happened as I was reading a small book on theology entitled *The Everlasting God* by D. Broughton Knox.

This is what I read:

> *The Father loves the Son and gives Him everything. The Son always does that which pleases the Father, The Spirit takes of the things of the Son and shows them to us. He does not glorify Himself. We learn from the Trinity that relationship is the essence of reality and therefore the essence of our existence, and we also learn that the way this relationship should be expressed is by concern for others. Within the Trinity itself there is a concern by the persons of the Trinity for one another.*[3]

That statement hit me with such spiritual force that it put me off my food for three days and has changed my whole view of God and people. I have no hesitation in saying that it affected my preaching, teaching and writing more than any other insight I have known.

Every part of that statement was powerful, but what impacted me most was the illuminating sentence:

> *We learn from the Trinity that relationship is the essence of Reality … and we also learn that the way this relationship should be expressed is by concern for others.*

You see, I had always been taught that truth was the essence of reality and ever since my days as a student I had always been on a search for truth, believing that to be the most important thing in the universe.

I wanted to know the truth about God, about life, about everything.

Now here comes a theologian who says the essence of reality is not truth but relationships. He is not minimising the importance of truth but pointing out that while truth is a reality – an important reality – ultimate reality is all about relationships.

C.S. Lewis puts it well when he says, 'Truth is always about something, but reality is that about which truth is.'

The other thing I saw from that powerful sentence was that the energy which pulses at the heart of the Trinity is other-centred.

> *... the way this relationship should be expressed is by concern for others. Within the Trinity itself there is a concern by the persons of the Trinity for one another.*

As I pondered those words I began to realise that the Trinity may well be motivated by other-centredness, but the motivation for my own life was one of sinful self-interest, the itch to prove that I could do it, the bid for attention, the desire for approval and so on.

I reflected on when I began my Christian ministry. When I took up my first pastorate I didn't think, 'What a wonderful thing it is to be able to serve so many people.' My thoughts were rather, 'What a wonderful thing it is to have a whole group of people, including deacons and elders, whom God has called to serve me.'

And now, years later, my attitude was basically the same. How wrong I had been. Why had it taken me so long to realise that I was there to serve them, not them to serve me?

As a result of pondering that powerful paragraph of D. Broughton Knox I began to experience deep changes. My fierce tendency to compete with others began to diminish; my insecure need to be recognised started to fade; my desire to win, always win, also began to fade and I came to see as Arthur Gordon put it that, 'As long as you feel you are serving others, you do the job well … when you are concerned with helping yourself you do it less well.'

I can recall the precise date when this paradigm shift took place and from that moment to this I have endeavoured with God's help to keep ever before me that I am here on the earth not to serve myself but to serve others.

THE LAW OF LOVE

The law I am talking about here – of being more interested in others than in oneself – is called in Scripture the law of love.

The apostle James calls it 'the royal law'. Here is how he puts it:

> *If you really keep the royal law found in Scripture, 'Love your neighbour as yourself,' you are doing right.*

> James 2:8

It is called 'royal' because it is the supreme law that is the source of all the laws governing human relationships. The apostle Paul makes it even clearer in his letter to the Romans where he says:

> *Let no debt remain outstanding, except the continuing debt to love one another, for he who loves his fellow-man has fulfilled the law. The commandments, 'Do not commit adultery,' 'Do not murder,' 'Do not steal,' 'Do not covet,' and whatever other commandment there may be, are summed up in this one rule: 'Love your neighbour as yourself.' Love does no harm to its neighbour. Therefore love is the fulfilment of the law.*

> Rom. 13:8–10

It was Jesus, of course, who first brought this truth into clear focus when, in answer to a lawyer's question, 'What is the greatest commandment?' He quoted with approval the Hebrew law:

> ' "*Love the Lord your God with all your heart and with all your soul and with all your mind." This is the first and greatest commandment. And the second is like it: "Love your neighbour as yourself." All the Law and the Prophets hang on these two commandments.*'
>
> Matt. 22:37–41

No Christian will have any difficulty in understanding the statement, 'You shall love the Lord your God with all your heart', but many I have found are confused by our Lord's next words: 'Love your neighbour as yourself.'

Based on a misunderstanding of these words, some teach that before you can love others you must learn to love yourself.

Believe it or not I know some churches (and I have preached in them) who instruct their people the proper order in relationships is this:

1. God
2. Yourself
3. Others

I quote from one such church's manual on the theme of 'Relationships' which says, 'After God you must put yourself next. You must learn to love yourself because unless you do you will never be able to love others in the way you should.'

People in this particular church are encouraged to get together in groups, for the purpose of learning to love themselves, and then go out and love others.

Now I readily admit that some people do not love themselves. In fact they hate themselves. They have been so badly damaged in their developmental years that they have chosen to adopt an attitude of self-rejection and self-humiliation.

Such people, however, are more the exception than the rule. Jesus is referring here to the attitude found in the hearts of all normal men and women – the healthy attitude of self-concern and self-love.

Our Lord's words spoken to the enquiring lawyer must be seen not simply as a statement, but as a command. Christ is making the point that, generally speaking, we all have a natural love for ourselves and a concern for our own survival and welfare. We all like to have a good home, a happy family, good health and so on. Jesus' point is that we ought also to seek that for others.

John Stott puts it like this:

Do you not like to satisfy your hunger? Then you must with similar urgency feed your neighbour. Jesus is presupposing not commanding love. We desire and seek what we think is for our own good and this universal trait becomes the rule by which all loving self-sacrifice must be measured.

So, to repeat, when Jesus said you should love your neighbour as yourself, He was referring to the attitude found in the hearts of all normal men and women – the healthy attitude of self-concern and self-love. Do you have difficulty with that?

Let me explain. Self-love is quite different from the love of self. Scripture recognises the legitimacy of self-love, just as long as it is not love *only* for the self, nor sought for its own sake, nor divorced from the equal love of others.

Love of self is where people are preoccupied with themselves, entirely self-centred, perhaps even narcissistic. This kind of love is condemned everywhere in Scripture.

The purpose of living, according to the statement Jesus made to the lawyer, then, is: loving involvement with God and loving involvement with others. And in John's Gospel Jesus makes it clear that the way He loves us is the way we are to love others. 'As I have loved you, so you must love one another' (John 13:34).

So before we can understand how to love others we must seek to grasp something of the nature of Christ's love for us; He is our model. The better we understand Him and follow in His footsteps the better we will be at loving as He loves.

WHAT IS LOVE?

I have come across many definitions and statements about love in my time. Here are some of my favourites:

'Love is bringing about the highest good in the life of another person.' (Charles Finney)

'Love is the only service that power cannot command and money cannot buy.' (Author unknown)

'Love and do what you will.' (Augustine of Hippo)

'Love is living, real living. Whoever loves true life will love true love.' (Author unknown)

'Love is always open arms. If you close your arms about love you'll find you are left holding yourself.' (Leo Busagle)

'To love another person is to help them love God.' (Søren Kierkagaard)

I think, however, that for me one of the most meaningful definitions of love I have ever come across – and one that gives a perspective we don't often think about – is the one given by C.S. Lewis. It's simple but so sublime:

To love is to be vulnerable.

When we love we give those we love the power to hurt us. And when someone hurts us we are prone to say to ourselves, 'Right, I will make sure I am never hurt like that again.'

One way we can protect ourselves from being hurt is to refuse to be vulnerable, to steel ourselves against other people and stop loving them.

My friend Dr Larry Crabb says that love is moving towards others without self-protection. We become vulnerable to hurt because we believe more in the power of love to hold us than the fear of rejection. Of course it hurts to love, but not to love hurts even more.

I find that whole concept – of moving towards others without self-protection – tremendously challenging. I have come to the conclusion, after close on six decades as a Christian, that although I know there are many things I can do well, what I do *least* well is to love as I am loved.

LOVING WELL

What does it mean to love well? It means that when your own heart is breaking you can still move towards others and be more interested in them than you are in yourself. This is where I have to put my hand on my heart and say that I am not very good at it. I have seen growth and development in this area over the years, but so often I grieve before my Lord that when it comes to loving as I am loved there are huge advances needed in my life.

The kind of love that Jesus has for us is a love that moves towards us even when He has been hurt by our indifference, our waywardness and by the many ways in which we withdraw from intimacy with Him.

Why are we so reluctant to move towards others without self-protection? Why do we find it so hard to be vulnerable? I believe one reason is because our lives are governed more by fear than by love.

'Perfect love,' we are told by the apostle John in his epistle, 'casts out fear.' When fear flows in love flows out. When love flows in fear flows out. It all depends on which power we expose our hearts to.

My reading tells me I am not alone in failing to love as I am loved. Eugene Peterson, whose paraphrase of the Bible (*The Message*) is one of the great achievements of modern days, tells very movingly of his struggle in this area.

> *Every day I put love on the line. There is nothing I am less good at than love. I am far better in competition than love. I am far better at responding to my instincts and ambitions to get ahead and make my mark than I am at figuring out how to love another.*
>
> *I am schooled and trained in acquisitive skills, in getting my own way. And yet, I decide every day to set aside what I can do best and attempt what I do very clumsily – open myself to the frustrations and failures of loving, daring to believe that failing in love is better than succeeding in pride.*[4]

The struggle to love well is not only from fear of being hurt or rejected, it's also because our human nature is shot through with self-centredness rather than other-centredness – the opposite of the Trinity. It is so easy to put your own interests before the interests of others.

ME FIRST!

Ever since I was a young man I have puzzled over the genesis of problems.
I like to understand as best I can the roots of issues. The Bible is the only
book that can help us trace the roots of self-centredness. To find its origins
we must go back, way back, to that ancient scene depicted for us in the
second and third chapters of Genesis.

What a perfect place it was back there in Eden, with rivers flowing
and animals bounding; but best of all, there was no sin. Adam and Eve
had a relationship that was free of problems. And because there was no
sin there was no selfishness. Until …

Soon after the devil entered the Garden with his enticing offer, Adam
and Eve surrendered to his temptation and as soon as sin took over in
their lives they immediately began to look out for number one.

God came down into the Garden and began to probe them with
some searching questions:

> *Then the man and his wife heard the sound of the LORD God as he was
> walking in the garden in the cool of the day, and they hid from the LORD
> God among the trees of the garden. But the LORD God called to the man,
> 'Where are you?' He answered, 'I heard you in the garden, and I was afraid
> because I was naked; so I hid.'*
> *And he said, 'Who told you that you were naked? Have you eaten from the
> tree from which I commanded you not to eat?'*
> *The man said, 'The woman you put here with me – she gave me some fruit
> from the tree, and I ate it.'*
> *Then the LORD God said to the woman, 'What is this you have done?'*
> *The woman said, 'The serpent deceived me, and I ate.'*
>
> Gen. 3:8–14

Notice how increasingly defensive Adam and Eve became as together they faced God's questions.

'The *woman* ...'
'The woman *you* gave me ...';
'The *serpent* ...'
'The serpent *deceived* me ...'

Has anything changed as we look at our own hearts in this, the twenty-first century? The truth is we caught the disease from Adam. It's a congenital illness in us all.

Ever since the days of Adam and Eve human nature has been smeared with marks of self-centredness and self-interest. If somehow we could eradicate self-centredness from the human heart there would be few relational problems.

Unwilling to face up to the fact that we are more interested in our own welfare than the welfare of others, we act like Adam and Eve in the Garden of Eden: we run, we hide, we deny, we shift the blame.

The first thing that must strike a Christian whenever he or she seriously conducts any kind of self-examination is how preoccupied we are with ourselves. In our fallen human nature everything seems to have an immediate self-reference. The instant reaction to any event is to think, 'How will this affect me?'

One man I knew, a preacher of the gospel, said that during a time of spiritual reflection he made a list of all the things he discovered in himself that were self-centred:

- *Diving for the best chair.*
- *Jumping the queue whenever possible.*
- *Monopolising the conversation.*

- *Boring others with talk about his grandchildren.*
- *Always wanting to get the best of a bargain.*

How chronic is this absorbing self-centredness!

Whenever I think of how easily self-interest can arise in our hearts, my mind goes back to a story I heard my father tell. A little boy came home from school one day to discover his pet goldfish lying stiff and motionless on the surface of the goldfish bowl. He was devastated and began to cry.

His father tried to console him by saying: 'It's sad when a pet dies, but here's what we will do. We'll put the dead little fish in a matchbox, take it out into the garden and invite your friends to join with us in conducting a funeral service. Then afterwards I will take you and your friends to the ice cream parlour and buy you all an ice cream.'

The little boy was cheered by this promise but suddenly he noticed that the goldfish was not dead as he had supposed, but had revived somehow and begun swimming merrily around the bowl. The little boy gave a whoop of joy, and clapped his hands in glee that his pet goldfish was still alive.

A few minutes later, however, he remembered the promise of his father to take him and his friends to the ice cream parlour. Now that would no longer be a possibility and he had mixed emotions – gladness that his goldfish was still alive, but sadness that he would miss out on a trip to the ice cream parlour. Eventually one emotion dominated the other and turning to his father said, 'Let's kill it.'

BECOMING OTHER-CENTRED

I said earlier that if we could eradicate self-centredness from the human heart there would be few relational problems. Well, it may not be possible to eradicate entirely the problem of self-centredness from our hearts, but I believe it is possible to diminish it.

Let me share with you some of the steps we need to take to turn from being a self-centred to an other-centred person. These are steps I try to follow every day of my life and I'm glad to report they are working.

THE SERVANT KING

The first thing we need to do, I suggest, is to focus on the fact that what our Saviour longs for every one of His children is that we might give ourselves to others in the same way that He gives Himself to us.

You are to love one another, He said, in the same way that I love you.

Jesus Christ was the only one who has ever lived on this earth completely free from self-centredness. Listen as He declares one of His primary reasons for coming to this world:

> *For even the Son of Man did not come to be served, but to serve, and to give his life as a ransom for many.*

> Mark 10:45

And again:

> *'I am among you as one who serves.'*

> Luke 22:27

No prevaricating. No fudging of the issue. He gives us in those words a crystal clear statement of why He is here. He came to serve and to give.

John Wesley said of our Lord, 'All his life was prayer and love.' We have only to study the Gospels to find Wesley's words confirmed. Jesus' first thought was not of Himself but to do His Father's will and His Father's will was one of costly serving of others.

The apostle Peter summarised our Saviour's life by saying, 'He went about doing good' (Acts 10:38). He fed the hungry, cheered the sad, preached good tidings to the poor.

One preacher said of Him, 'In Jesus Christ there moved on the surface of this planet for the only time in history a completely *unself-centred* person. Comb the record of his days on earth and you will find nothing on which you can convict him of selfishness.' Wesley was right: 'All His life was prayer and love.'

It makes sense then that the one who so brilliantly modelled the other-centredness of the Trinity desires that our lives should be run in the same way. What He longs for us is that we might do it too. It was the thought in the last prayer He uttered in John 17:

> *'May they be brought to complete unity to let the world know that you sent me and have loved them even as you have loved me.'*
>
> John 17:23

But nowhere is the willingness and desire and attitude of our Lord to serve seen better than in that passage in John 13:1–17.

While in the first century Rome was famous for its paved roads, in the rest of the world they were few and far between. Roads were little more than winding dust trails and it was the custom for hosts to provide a slave at the door of each home to wash the feet of guests as they arrived.

The servant would kneel with a pitcher of water, a pan and a towel and wash the dirt from the feet of those who entered the home. Shoes and sandals were left at the door, a custom still prevalent in the Middle and Far East. If a home could not afford a slave then either one of the guests would perform the service, or one of the family.

How interesting that here, none of the guests had volunteered for the lowly task. The room was filled with proud hearts. They were willing to fight for a throne but not for a towel. Now read carefully the account of what transpired:

Jesus knew that the Father had put all things under his power, and that he had come from God and was returning to God; so he got up from the meal, took off his outer clothing, and wrapped a towel round his waist. After that, he poured water into a basin and began to wash his disciples' feet, drying them with the towel that was wrapped around him.

He came to Simon Peter, who said to him, 'Lord, are you going to wash my feet?'

Jesus replied, 'You do not realise now what I am doing, but later you will understand.'

'No,' said Peter, 'you shall never wash my feet.'

Jesus answered, 'Unless I wash you, you have no part with me.'

'Then, Lord,' Simon Peter replied, 'not just my feet but my hands and my head as well!'

Jesus answered, 'A person who has had a bath needs only to wash his feet; his whole body is clean. And you are clean, though not every one of you.'

John 13:3–10

Look into the mirror of Christ and contrast His attitudes and actions with yours. Would you have done that? It's one thing to read it and to examine it but it's another to decide to follow it. 'I left you an example,' He said, 'that you should do these things.'

A poem I came across puts it beautifully:

You know, Lord, how I serve You,
With great emotional fervour;
In the limelight.
You know how eagerly I speak for You
At a woman's club.
You know how I effervesce when I promote
A fellowship group.
You know my genuine enthusiasm
At a Bible study.

But how would I react, I wonder,
If you pointed to a basin of water
And asked me to wash the calloused feet
Of a bent and wrinkled old woman –
Day after day,
Month after month,
In a room where nobody saw
And nobody knew.

Ruth Harms Cullim

CHOOSE TO SERVE

The second thing we need to realise is this: that although we are tainted with self-centredness we can *choose* to live otherwise.

No sooner does the life of God come into the soul of any man or woman through conversion than that life seeks to manifest itself in the same way that it revealed itself in Jesus Christ. The only thing that blocks it is our pride and unwillingness. We must trample on our pride and seek to rise above it.

On one occasion in the Gospels Jesus pulls aside His disciples and spells out the sharp contrast between His philosophy and the system of the day:

> *Jesus called them together and said, 'You know that the rulers of the Gentiles lord it over them, and their high officials exercise authority over them. Not so with you. Instead, whoever wants to become great among you must be your servant, and whoever wants to be first must be your slave – just as the Son of Man did not come to be served, but to serve, and to give his life as a ransom for many.'*
>
> Matt. 20:25–28

In the world's system there are different levels of authority. It was true in the time of Jesus and it's true also today. In government there is a prime minister, republics have a president. In the military there are officers and enlisted men and women. In sport there are coaches and trainers. In the business world there are heads of corporations, managers, under managers and so on. That's how the system works. As Jesus said, 'their high officials exercise authority over them.'

But Jesus challenged His disciples by saying, 'Not so with you.' Or, in other words, that's not the way I want it to be among My disciples.

Jesus impressed upon His disciples the fact that, though they had been afflicted with the Adam-and-Eve disease they were no longer to operate like that; they were to renounce the old attitudes of the past and to follow His example.

And what was that example? Serving others as opposed to serving self. The apostle Paul, when writing of Christ's example, said:

> *Do nothing out of selfish ambition or vain conceit, but in humility consider others better than yourselves. Each of you should look not only to your own interests, but also to the interests of others. Your attitude should be the same as that of Christ Jesus.*

> Phil. 2:3–5

How different is the counsel we get from the secular world! J.B. Phillips, in his book, *When God was Man*, illustrates the attitude of the world when he changes the Beatitudes to read thus:

> *Happy are the 'pushy' for they get on in the world.*
> *Happy are the hard-boiled, for they never let life hurt them.*
> *Happy are they who complain, for they get their own way in the end.*
> *Happy are the blasé, for they never worry over their sins.*
> *Happy are the slave drivers, for they get results.*
> *Happy are the knowledgeable of the world for they know their way around.*
> *Happy are the troublemakers, for they make people take notice of them.*[5]

Those words are, of course, the complete opposite of what our Lord said in His Sermon on the Mount, recorded for us in Matthew chapter 5. There He laid down the proposition that life – true life – is found in giving not getting, being more interested in others than in oneself.

There is not enough space in this chapter to bring together all the biblical texts I would like to focus on so I have chosen some of the more well-known passages:

Be devoted to one another in brotherly love. Honour one another above yourselves. Never be lacking in zeal, but keep your spiritual fervour, serving the Lord. Be joyful in hope, patient in affliction, faithful in prayer. Share with God's people who are in need. Practise hospitality.

Rom. 12:10–13

You, my brothers, were called to be free. But do not use your freedom to indulge the sinful nature; rather, serve one another in love.

Gal. 5:13

Therefore, as we have opportunity, let us do good to all people, especially to those who belong to the family of believers.

Gal. 6:10

For we are God's workmanship, created in Christ Jesus to do good works, which God prepared in advance for us to do.

Eph. 2:10

Command those who are rich in this present world not to be arrogant nor to put their hope in wealth, which is so uncertain, but to put their hope in God, who richly provides us with everything for our enjoyment. Command them to do good, to be rich in good deeds, and to be generous and willing to share.

1 Tim. 6:17–18

And do not forget to do good and to share with others, for with such sacrifices God is pleased.

Heb. 13:16

Anyone, then, who knows the good he ought to do and doesn't do it, sins.
James 4:17

'In the same way, let your light shine before men, that they may see your good deeds and praise your Father in heaven.'

Matt. 5:16

These are just some of the scriptures that point to the fact that we who are Christians are expected to be engaged in ministering to and serving others. And there are many more. There is power in God's Word and as you read it it will penetrate your soul with its challenge. Scripture constantly cuts across our preconceived ideas to challenge the selfishness rooted in our carnal nature. But we need to be challenged if we are to change.

LOVING AND GIVING

The third thing is this: Begin to think of ways in which you can minister to others in love. Tilt your soul in the direction of serving rather than being served, of giving rather than receiving. Develop an attitude of giving. All actions begin with the right attitude. Everyone has their favourite scripture and this is the one, which I quoted before, that I turn to regularly:

Do nothing out of selfish ambition or vain conceit, but in humility consider others better than yourselves. Each of you should look not only to your own interests, but also to the interests of others.
Your attitude should be the same as that of Christ Jesus:

Who, being in very nature God,

   did not consider equality with God something to be grasped,

but made himself nothing,

   taking the very nature of a servant,

   being made in human likeness.

Phil. 2:3–7

A friend of mine in the Far East, a Malaysian Christian who lives in Kuala Lumpur, always gives me a small gift whenever he meets me. It might be a set of cuff links, or a diary, or some handkerchiefs; but he always gives me something.

When I asked him why he did this, he told me this story:

I used to be preoccupied only with myself. I would look to others to give to me and rarely would I consider what I might do for others. God spoke to me about this in a moving sermon by one of the pastors in our church and it turned my life upside down. I realised that life is more about giving than getting and I committed myself to blessing as many people I can every day of my life.

One of the things he likes to do is to go into a confectionery shop and buy a small selection of their best cakes and pastries. Then he waits outside and prays that God will guide him to someone who needs a cheerful word and an act of encouragement.

He will say to such a person, 'Your heavenly Father has told me to give you this. God loves you and so do I.' Then he walks away.

A rather remarkable thing happened after one of these encounters. He was sitting in his local church some months later and heard a woman giving her testimony of how she came to Christ. She said, 'I was feeling very suicidal one day as I had very little money and everything seemed to be going wrong in my life. Then a man stepped out of a confectionery shop, handed me a bag of the most wonderful pastries and said, "Your heavenly Father has told me to give you this. God loves you and so do I."

'This made such an impression on me that I sought out a neighbour who I knew was a Christian and asked her if she would introduce me to her church. The first time I attended I heard how Jesus Christ had died for me and I received Him into my life as my Lord and Saviour.'

As he listened to her testimony my friend remembered her face and when the testimony service was over he went up to her and said, 'I was that man.' As they talked the woman asked him, 'After you had given me the gift why didn't you ask me if I would like to become a Christian?'

His reply was classic: 'My motive,' he said, 'was not to save you but to bless you. What follows from that I confidently left in the hands of God.'

Early one chilly winter morning in London during the Second World War a soldier was making his way to the barracks and spotted a lad with his nose pressed against the window of a baker's shop.

Inside the baker was kneading dough for a fresh supply of doughnuts. The hungry boy stared in silence watching every move. The soldier walked over to the shop and stood at the side of the little boy.

Through the steamed-up window he could see the mouth-watering items that were being pulled from the oven. They watched as the baker put them in a glass enclosed counter.

The soldier's heart went out to the little boy. He said, 'Son, would you like some of those doughnuts?' The boy was startled. 'Yes, I would,' he said. The soldier stepped inside the shop, bought a few of the doughnuts and walked back to where the lad was.

He smiled as he held out the bag and said simply, 'They're yours.' He walked away but he hadn't got far when he felt a tug at his coat. He looked down and heard the child ask quietly, 'Mister, are you Jesus?'

We are never more like Jesus than when we give ourselves to others. It's the law by which every one of us should live.

Law 6
STAY CLOSE TO GOD

Sc

TURN TO GOD

It is just as it was when you passed it before, but your eyes
are altered. You see nothing now but realities. (C.S. Lewis)

There seem to be few real prophets in today's Church. The late Vance Havner, a quaint old American preacher, used to say that the contemporary Christian Church is very much a non-prophet organisation.

One man I have a great admiration for and whom I regard as a modern-day prophet is Charles Colson. A former White House assistant during Richard Nixon's reign, Colson went to prison for his involvement in the Watergate scandal, but since his conversion to Jesus Christ and aided by the Holy Spirit he has brought his high-powered perception to bear upon spiritual things.

It was on 12 August 1973 that Colson first felt the claims of Jesus Christ on his soul. He had just spent time with Tom Phillips, President of the Raytheon Company, the largest employer in New England.

Phillips shared with Colson the story of how he had come to Christ and sensing Chuck's interest read him a chapter from C.S. Lewis's book *Mere Christianity* – a chapter about pride. As he heard Lewis's words the tough politician felt them biting into his conscience. His view of himself began to change as he saw himself as he really was.

> *Suddenly I felt naked and unclean, my bravado defences gone. I was*
> *exposed, unprotected, for Lewis's words were describing me ... Just as*
> *a man about to die is supposed to see flash before him, sequence by*
> *sequence, the high points of his life, so as Tom's voice read on that August*
> *evening, key events in my life paraded before me.*[1]

Later that evening Colson got into his car and as he groped for the ignition key he found himself caught up in a wave of deep emotion. He was not quite sure what was happening to him and so he got out of his car to go back into Tom Phillips's house. However, he saw the lights being extinguished one by one and so he returned to his car and started the engine.

What happened then is best told in his own words:

As I drove out of Tom's driveway, the tears were flowing uncontrollably ... I was crying so hard it was like trying to swim underwater. Then came the strange sensation that water was not only running down my cheeks, but surging through my whole body as well, cleansing and cooling as it went. They weren't tears of sadness or remorse, nor of joy – but somehow tears of relief. And then I prayed my first real prayer: 'God, I don't know how to find You, but I'm going to try. I'm not much the way I am now, but somehow I want to give myself to You.' I didn't know how to say more so I repeated over and over the words 'Take me.' I stayed there in the car, wet-eyed, praying, thinking for perhaps half an hour, perhaps longer, alone in the quiet of the dark night. Yet for the first time in my life I was not alone at all.[2]

Some have thought that Colson experienced a nervous breakdown or burnout that night in Tom Phillips's driveway. Subsequent events show this not to be so. What actually happened was that he found himself in the throes of repentance – the spiritual revolution that takes place in the soul when one begins to realise one's need to find forgiveness for sin and turn one's life over to God.

REPENTANCE

What I most admire about Charles Colson is his strong and clear emphasis on repentance, not just as the entry into the Christian life, *but as a way of developing and improving in the Christian life*. It is this emphasis that in my opinion contributes to marking him out as one of this generation's great prophets.

Read carefully this quotation from a section of his writings.

> *The repentance God desires of us is not just contrition over particular sins; it is also a daily attitude, a perspective ... it is the process by which we see ourselves, day by day, as we really are, sinful, needy, dependent people. It is the process by which we see God as He is, awesome majestic holy ... and it so radically alters our perspective that we begin to see the world through God's eyes not our own. Repentance is the ultimate surrender of the self.*[3]

This concept of repentance being not only the way we enter the Christian life but also a daily attitude, a daily perspective, is something that seems to be missing among this modern generation.

Most Christians I talk to view repentance as a one-off event, something they did when they were converted and need never repeat. Time and time again whenever I have suggested to believers that repentance ought to be a regular occurrence in the Christian life they have looked at me blankly and said, 'But I did that when I was converted.'

Let's examine this issue of repentance first as the doorway into the Christian life and then as a daily attitude and perspective. I invite you to do so because I consider the issue of repentance to be a law of the spiritual life as sure and as certain as the others I have mentioned.

THE WAY IN

The word repentance comes from the Greek word *metanoia* which means a change of mind. Several other states of mind can easily be mistaken for repentance, so before proceeding any further it may be well, as far as possible, to clear away any misunderstandings.

Repentance is not regret. Regret is being sorry for oneself, deploring the consequences of one's actions but not necessarily making a change.

Repentance is not remorse. Remorse is sorrow without hope at its heart; it is an emotion of disgust. It eats its heart out instead of seeking a new heart.

Repentance is not reformation. Reformation (changing one's way of life) may follow repentance, but it can never precede it.

Repentance is not reparation. Reparation or restitution is practical proof of the reality of repentance but it must not be mistaken for repentance.

I am afraid that what often passes for repentance in the Christian community is not real repentance at all; it is only remorse or regret. And one of the tragedies in contemporary Christian circles (in my view) is that there are many people sitting in our churches who regard themselves as Christians but who have never experienced true repentance.

On one of my trips to India I heard a man say that when he was a boy he watched a butterfly as it struggled out of its cocoon. The sticky strands of goo seemed to prevent its exit so, desirous of helping it, he ran back to his house, got hold of a pair of scissors, cut away the strands and helped the butterfly emerge. He was amazed when the butterfly lay on the ground unable to fly – his 'help' had produced a cripple, incapable of flight.

He learned later that the struggle of metamorphosis is necessary to the insect's ability to fly and without that struggle the butterfly's wings can never develop properly. 'Christians who have never known repentance,' says John White, 'are like butterflies that have never flown.'[4]

How sad that so many cannot 'fly' in the Christian life because the process by which they became Christians did not involve true repentance. We do men and women a disservice when we try to make it easy for them to enter the Christian life.

I heard an evangelist say on one occasion, 'I have a card here for you to sign. Just sign it where it says, "Today I have become a Christian" and your name will be transferred to the Lamb's book of life, which will entitle you in the eternal kingdom to a mansion in the skies and perhaps even to be a ruler over ten cities when Christ returns.'

In his sermon he had not said a word about the necessity of repentance or the need to turn away from sin. I wondered as I watched the thirty or forty people who went forward that night how many of them would 'fly'.

Churches have different approaches to introducing people to the Christian life. Some give a few basic facts about the work that Christ accomplished on the cross and invite people to believe on Him.

Others baptise infants and expect them when they come to an age of understanding to be confirmed in the faith.

And there are others who, having built up strong feelings through music and emotionally charged stories, rely on these to break down people's resistance to Christ and turn over their lives to Him.

I am not saying that these methods do not result in some people becoming Christians but I am saying that where *there is no genuine repentance there can be no ongoing and developing relationship with God.*

In the counselling room I have had the privilege of leading many through the process of deep repentance. They may have become Christians through one of the 'systems' described above, but many of them have said to me afterwards, 'It was from that moment that I really mark the beginning of my Christian experience.'

EARTHQUAKE IN THE SOUL

Where there is no struggle to face the appalling fact of inbred sin, no mourning over our stubborn commitment to independence, there will be less subsequent joy and rapture in the soul and less possibility of a great change in character.

'Repentance,' says Dr John White, 'is a changed way of looking at things.'[5] He defines repentance as the shock that comes from seeing reality. It is a terrible thing to claim to be a Christian and yet to live independently of the life offered to us in Christ, to relegate God to irrelevance. The full realisation of that, brought about by the Holy Spirit, can, says John White, be like an earthquake in the soul.

Without this inner revolution, this earthquake in the soul, nothing deep and profound happens in a person's spiritual life.

This is what did happen to Charles Colson on Tom Phillips's porch. A spiritual earthquake took place and his view of things suddenly changed. He saw himself as he really was – not a consummate professional but a desperately needy soul in need of forgiveness and a new view of reality.

It's worth considering Colson's words one more time:

Suddenly I felt naked and unclean, my bravado defences gone. I was exposed, unprotected, for Lewis's words were describing me ... Just as a man about to die is supposed to see flash before him, sequence by sequence, the high points of his life, so as Tom's voice read on that August evening, key events in my life paraded before me.[6]

There can be no great change in the soul if there is no change in the way we see things. Colson saw himself in those moments in a different light, facing truths about himself that he had denied earlier. His view of reality changed and so later did his character.

A NEW VIEW

If repentance is a new view of reality then what kind of reality are we talking about? In this postmodern generation there are people who say *any* reality is valid if it's 'real for you'. This means that reality is subjective.

As a Christian I believe that anyone who denies the fact of God's existence and the fact that we live in a moral universe is really denying reality. Reality is not subjective but objective. God has given us a body of truth in the Bible which tells us all we need to know about how to run our lives effectively. Anyone who refuses to face that fact is, in my view, not a realist but a retreatist.

One definition of repentance I have often used, but which is not original to me is this: 'Repentance is a revulsion against sin resulting from a revelation of the righteousness and love of God.'

A text that comes to mind in this connection is found in Paul's letter to the Romans: 'God's kindness leads you towards repentance' (Rom. 2:4).

When we see how good God is in providing us in Christ with all the resources we need to live the life He has designed us to live on this earth, any awareness of how we may be ignoring that fact creates (or should create) a sorrow that leads to repentance (2 Cor. 7:9).

We began our chapter with C.S. Lewis's definition of repentance as a new way of seeing things. 'It is just as it was when you passed it before,' he says, 'but your eyes are altered. You see nothing now but realities.'

Charles Finney wrote, 'To one who truly repents sin looks like a different thing from what it does to him who has not repented.'

The entrance into the Christian life is through the door of repentance. The term I know has a harsh sound in modern ears. People would gladly cut it out of the religious vocabulary if they could. But there it stands. It humbles men and women's pride. It rebukes self-complacency. It tells us that there is something radically wrong with our lives. It summons us to submit to the righteousness which is of God through faith in Jesus Christ.

If a person does not repent what happens? Jesus Christ leaves us in no doubt. Speaking to a group of people following an accident when the tower of Siloam fell and eighteen people were killed, He said that although they did not die because they were more sinful than others, 'Unless you repent, you too will all perish' (Luke 13:3).

Is that not an accurate description of what actually takes place in the soul of a person who refuses to repent? Bit by bit he or she perishes. An inevitable process of deterioration sets in.

The apostle Peter picked up this theme of his Master when, speaking by the Spirit on the Day of Pentecost, he said:

> '*Repent and be baptised, every one of you, in the name of Jesus Christ for the forgiveness of your sins. And you will receive the gift of the Holy Spirit.*'
>
> Acts 2:38

THE WAY TO LIVE

Having seen repentance is the prerequisite for entering the Christian life, we now consider its place in the improvement and development of the Christian life.

In this respect, let me remind you of Colson's words one more time:

The repentance God desires of us is not just contrition over particular sins; it is also a daily attitude, a perspective.

Colson is right when he says that repentance is not just contrition over particular sins. It is that of course but it is also the process by which we see ourselves, day by day, as we really are, sinful, needy, dependent people.

It is so easy to move away from depending on Christ to make our lives work. As a friend of mine puts it, 'We can come into the Christian life through the door of radical repentance but then when we are in we attempt to live the life God has called us to in our own strength.'

Christians who fail to see themselves as desperately needy and dependent people, requiring the resources of Christ to flow through them in order to live life as He planned it, have not begun to grasp what the Christian life is all about.

Although there are a number of Bible passages that underline the fact we should see ourselves as needy and dependent people, one of the most powerful is in John 15.

'Abide in Me and I in you. As the branch cannot bear fruit of itself, unless it abides in the vine, neither can you, unless you abide in Me. I am the vine, you are the branches. He who abides in Me, and I in him, bears much fruit; for without Me you can do nothing. If anyone does not abide in Me, he is cast out as a branch and is withered; and they gather them and throw them into the fire, and they are burned. If you abide in Me, and My words abide in you, you will ask what you desire, and it shall be done for you. By this My Father is glorified, that you bear much fruit; so you will be My disciples.'

John 15:4–8, NKJV

The reason I have selected the New King James Version above as opposed to the NIV is because it uses the word 'abide'. The NIV says 'Remain in me'. As a lover of words I feel the word 'abide' is a much more appropriate word than 'remain'. It has a certain ring about it that the word 'remain' lacks.

'ABIDE IN ME'

Early in my ministry, when I was worn out by a certain spiritual battle I was going through, I remember reading those words of our Lord: 'Abide in Me and I in you and you shall ask what you will, and it shall be done for you.'

I said, 'Lord, why am I feeling the way I do when I am abiding in You and Your Spirit is in me?' The impression came, 'You are not abiding in Me. You are abiding in something else.'

Those words rang in my ears for days and led to some hours of soul searching. I discovered in those hours that living for God requires much more than just doing good works or not sinning; it requires confidence and trust.

I asked myself, if I am not abiding in Jesus then where am I abiding? I began to put down on paper some of the thoughts and sentences that were going around in my head. Sometimes these thoughts were just below the level of consciousness, but there were moments when I was aware of them nevertheless.

They were thoughts like this: 'I am working so hard and giving myself to the ministry with such enthusiasm, why don't more people recognise this and compliment me?'

Then I would move to another level and find the thought circulating inside my head: 'People are so disappointing, you just can't depend on them to come through for you.' And then I would cynically say to myself, 'Blow them! Why should I care?'

SOUL PAIN KILLERS

The surprising thing is that when I reached a cynical level I felt better. From my abiding place of cynicism I felt free to take some soul pain killers – things that would allow me to feel better for a while.

And what were those pain killers? A late night film on television, perhaps, with just enough sexual titillation to provide distraction without at the same time making me feel thoroughly unsanctified.

Or deliberately provoking an argument with my wife – an argument I would invariably win because I was better at words than she.

How I relished those arguments! They gave me a feeling of superiority and acted like an anodyne to the pain that was in my soul. Cynicism was my main abiding place, my comforter. These things became what John Eldridge calls 'Other lovers for my soul'.

It is so easy to sing, 'Jesus, Lover of my soul' but then, when the soul is in pain, to turn to other lovers. By going to these other abiding places I was filling my heart with things that made the emptiness go away for a moment.

Eugene Peterson's paraphrase, *The Message*, was not in existence at that time but if it had been I would have read Jesus' words in this way:

> *'If you make yourselves at home with me and my words are at home in you, you can be sure that whatever you ask will be listened to and acted upon.'*

John 15:7

My problem was that Jesus had made His home in me but I was not making my home within Him. My abiding place was not in the Lord but in cynicism. There were other abiding places I was resting in too, but none so attractive as cynicism. It was a lot easier to make my life work by seeking the help of these other comforters than by trusting Christ Himself.

How was this matter resolved? Through the simple act of repentance. My prayer went something like this.

Heavenly Father, forgive me for so foolishly trying to meet my needs in my own way when I see that You and You alone are to be my supply. I repent of my tendency to make my life work independently of You and ask Your forgiveness for my stubborn and arrogant refusal to trust You with my life. Help me, Lord Jesus, to turn to You in daily dependency and draw from You, the uniquely sufficient God, all I need to hold my life together. In Christ's name.
Amen.

One of the things I have discovered in looking into my own heart and into the hearts of others who have come to me for counselling is that there are many comforters, or abiding places, that we turn to when our souls are in pain. Things like

- money
- success
- self-pity
- rebellion
- physical appearance

These things, and others like them, are illusions. They cannot bring life. Life is found only in Jesus Christ.

The Old Testament uses another metaphor to describe our tendency to turn to things other than God to make our lives work:

'Be appalled at this, O heavens,

   and shudder with great horror,' declares the LORD.

'My people have committed two sins:

They have forsaken me,

   the spring of living water,

and have dug their own cisterns,

   broken cisterns that cannot hold water.'

Jer. 2:12–13

In this remarkable passage God is so concerned about something that He calls the heavens to come and look at what His people are doing. And what are they doing? These thirsty people walked right by the water God provided for their souls, grabbed a shovel and went out into the desert to dig their own wells.

Why would people spurn a fresh spring of water? It doesn't make sense. Why did they choose dirty, lukewarm, bacteria infested water (metaphorically speaking) when they could slake their thirst at a pure spring? And the wells they dug sprung leaks every time. The people got a few mouthfuls of water and then it was gone. Then they go and dig another one. How ridiculous!

There are two sins in this passage: they have forsaken the Lord, and they have dug their own cisterns.

EVERYONE IS THIRSTY

The assumption in the text is that everyone is thirsty. It is not spelled out, but it can be safely assumed. Remember, God never condemns us for being thirsty; He condemns us for trying to satisfy our thirst in other ways than Himself.

Our problem is that deeply rooted in our souls is a strong desire for independence. We want to be in control of satisfying our own thirst. The energy behind our well-digging is this: we will do whatever it takes to provide ourselves with feelings that give us a sense of wellbeing.

This fallen world is like a desert that does not give entire satisfaction and thus our souls are parched. So what do we do? Do we humbly draw near to God and drink from His life-giving stream in glad and utter dependency? No, that would make us feel helpless and powerless.

As our carnal nature abhors the feeling of helplessness, we take our shovels and spades and begin to dig wells of our own making, hoping to find water.

Whether we think in terms of 'abiding places' or 'digging wells' one thing is clear – there is a tendency in us all to try and make our lives work independently of God. And this tendency is embedded like splintered glass in our souls.

'Progress in the Christian life,' said W.L. Rowlands, a famous Welsh Bible teacher of a generation ago, 'is determined by how well we understand the difference between trust and independence.'

He added: 'We should ask ourselves regularly (daily would be best) where is my dependency? Given that is your sincere prayer God will soon show you whether your life is hid with Christ in God or you are depending on your own resources to make your life work.'

RETURN TO THE LORD

Whenever we feel ourselves moving away from dependency on Christ and leaning on other things, then we must recognise that our misplaced dependency is sin, confess it and repent of it.

It is only when we do this that we can grow and develop into the person God meant us to be and experience the realisation of our full personhood.

Here is how a friend of mine put it after having flown from Nashville to the UK to attend a Christ Empowered Living seminar:

> *For years I felt condemned by the words 'Repent, for the kingdom of God is at hand'. Then I attended your Christ Empowered Living seminar and everything changed. It taught me that my view of God was coloured by my worldview of myself, not by the truth.*
>
> *If I am honest, I viewed God as someone who was after my obedience and not my friendship. Now I know that true repentance is always positive, because I have a God who is caring and loving. To understand the true meaning of repentance is to understand the true meaning of the Christian life. I learned that repentance is a lifestyle. It's turning towards something that is good – daily. Just as I want to eat daily, so I want to repent daily. I find the more I repent, the cleaner I feel inside and the more I want to know God. Quiet times are becoming less of a duty and more of a joy. Now I look forward to hanging out with God. I always knew I had problems but I never knew how to fix them. I finally learned how when I attended Christ Empowered Living. My entire understanding (mentally and emotionally) of God has taken a 180 degree turn.*

But how do we go about the task of repenting? Let me go back to another Old Testament passage which is probably the best for depicting what is involved in repentance. I am indebted to Dr Larry Crabb for drawing my attention to these verses:

> *Return, O Israel, to the LORD your God.*
> *Your sins have been your downfall!*
> *Take words with you*
> *and return to the LORD.*

Say to him:

    'Forgive all our sins

and receive us graciously,

    that we may offer the fruit of our lips.

Assyria cannot save us;

    we will not mount war-horses.

We will never again say, "Our gods" to what our own hands have made,

    for in you the fatherless find compassion.'

Hos. 14:1–3

Let your thoughts go over these important words once again: *'Return to the LORD your God. Your sins have been your downfall.'* Sin is best seen as a movement away from God. And any departure from God requires an act of repentance that results in a 180° turn in God's direction. A 90° turn is not enough. It means a right-about turn; to quote C.S. Lewis again: 'Repentance is a movement full speed astern.'

'Take words with you and return to the LORD.' This means clarifying to ourselves and God exactly what we are repenting of and what we wish to happen. There must be no fumbling of the issue.

In my own life I have found a regular need to identify three things which are ever-present in my life and need regularly to be repented of:

A failure to trust God with my longings.

A failure to believe His evaluation of my worth.

A failure to see that because He is in it my life has a special meaning and purpose.

'Return to the LORD' again underlines the fact that true repentance is a coming back to God.

'*Your sins have been your downfall.*' We must always be willing to call sin by its rightful name and to see it for what it is. There must be no euphemisms, no tampering with the labels. To spurn God's grace and rely instead on our own resources is not merely a spiritual infraction, it is sin.

'*Receive us graciously that we may offer the fruit of our lips.*' The purpose of repentance is that we might worship and live for God in the way He desires, daily dependent on His grace. Under the old covenant an animal sacrifice was made to atone for sin, but what God longed for was a sacrifice of praise arising from a realised awareness of forgiveness. Where this attitude of thankfulness for sins forgiven is absent there can be no true worship.

'*Assyria cannot save us.*' Assyria was a nation that had become an international power during the time of Hosea's writings. But for the nation of Israel to look to them when they needed help, rather than putting their trust in the living God was, Hosea says, not an option.

'*We will not mount war-horses.*' Israel was expected not to trust in chariots and horses (Psa. 20:7), but in the power and provision of the Great El-Shaddai, 'the nourisher and sustainer of His people'.

'*We will never again say, "Our gods" to what our own hands have made.*' Their confidence was not to be put in the works their hands had made. It is one thing to enjoy the things our hands have made; it is quite another to worship them.

'*In you the fatherless find compassion.*' Only in God can be found the compassion our souls long for. A person who repents stops using his own hands or the works of his hands to gain compassion. Rather they bring their deepest needs to God and trust Him for their soul's satisfaction.

Repentance really is a mindset that looks to God for life and does not rest or rely on one's own expertise, degrees, academic achievements or business acumen. It is not that we cannot enjoy the fruits of our labours, but we must not draw our life from them.

Our lives are hid with Christ in God, says Paul. So there must be a turning from all self-reliance that we have depended on to make our lives work.

I hope it is clear now. Repentance is turning back to God. Returning to Him for the second or the twenty-second time may be challenging but there is no other way to profound and positive change. This is what one writer has to say about repentance:

> *Repentance, this willing submission of humiliation and a kind of death, is not something God demands of you before He will take you back and which he could let you off if He chose; it is simply a description of what going back to Him is like. If you ask God to take you back without it you are really asking Him to let you go back without going back. It cannot happen.*

If our repentance contains only regret, remorse and reformation; if we are sorry not that we have misplaced our dependency but that we have lost our inner peace; if we are sorry only because we have found our spirit clouded with guilt, then our repentance is not really repentance at all.

The biggest problem we face in our Christian lives, and one we must always be ready to face, is the fact that we tend to rely on our own resources to make our lives work rather than depending on the strength and grace that comes from God.

This is what I mean by repentance being ongoing. We may not commit sins like fornication, adultery, stealing, cheating and so on but it is no less a sin to turn to some other source of comfort or to dig our own wells.

DAILY REPENTANCE

Can there be any doubt that repentance is a law of the soul? You enter the

Christian life through repentance and you improve it the same way. No repentance – no ongoing progress. It's as simple and as sublime as that.

Someone once asked me, 'Doesn't this emphasis on the need for daily repentance lead to a negative view of life?' My answer to that question was this: 'It can do, if you hold within you a concept of God that is negative. If you see God as someone who is only interested in getting you to live right rather than someone who longs to be in a right relationship with you then repentance will be something you enter into reluctantly rather than freely.'

There are some who believe repentance is exclusively a human matter. I heard one such advocate of that view put it like this: 'I see the folly of my ways, and I make up my mind to change. That is repentance. It begins with me and ends with God.'

I prefer to think of repentance as reaching out for something that God initiates. And I think Scripture supports that view. Paul talks about the necessity for Timothy to gently instruct those who opposed him 'in the hope that God will grant them repentance leading them to a knowledge of the truth' (2 Tim. 2:25). Note the phrase 'in the hope that God will *grant* them repentance'.

GOD'S INITIATIVE

How does God grant us repentance? What is the Almighty's involvement in this?

I think this is what it means. When I allow myself to focus on the central truth I have been trying to convey in this chapter, namely, that Jesus Christ wants to occupy the central place in our hearts, the Holy Spirit stands by eager and ready to bring us to the place of repentance.

There is a wonderful moment in C.S. Lewis's fictional work *Perelandra* which powerfully illuminates what I am trying to say here.

The hero, Ransom, arrives on the planet Venus to discover that the surface is largely ocean, dotted with floating islands. On one of the islands Ransom meets a woman who is a sort of Eve character – a strange blend of innocence and curiosity. By some mishap she has been separated from her husband and in the conversation with Ransom she says:

> *I thought that I was carried in the will of him I love, but now I see I walk with it. I thought that the good things he sent me drew me into them as the waves lift the islands, but now I see that it is I who plunge into them with my own legs and arms, as when we go swimming.*[7]

God wants us to plunge into the waves He sends us. We are not to sit passively but to take advantage of the grace that flows towards us and respond to what is willed. From one perspective it might seem repentance begins with others; from another it begins with God. The truth is perhaps that the human and the divine are so close in co-operation that one cannot tell where one ends and the other begins.

For me the classic illustration of repentance being the means of returning to God and being close to Him once again is the story of the church in Ephesus, recorded for us in the book of Revelation.

The church at Ephesus, despite their spiritual industriousness, had moved away from a close and intimate relationship with the Lord and the only way back was through the door of repentance.

Christ, the Wonderful Counsellor, lays before them the three things that need to be done when our relationship with God is fractured: remember, repent and return. But notice before the Church is commanded to return to doing 'the things you did at first' Christ commands them to repent.

There is no point in doing the right things unless one is sorry for the things that have drawn us away from Him. Otherwise we simply become moralists, doing all the right things but with our hearts far away from God.

It is generally agreed by spiritual directors and all who have the care of souls that the grace of repentance is an essential prerequisite in any heart that would be open to divine influence and that without it, God can hardly begin to have His way in a life.

Not only is it necessary theologically, it is necessary practically. God justly requires repentance in mortals because the Deity can never condone sin. Only repentant hearts are truly teachable and ready to profit by the bitter experiences that sin brings.

Learning the art of constantly turning to God doesn't mean that we live in a state of nervous tension. I like the words of Oswald Chambers in this regard: 'In the initial stages it is a continual effort, until it becomes so much the law of life that you abide in him unconsciously.'

Charles Colson was right. The ultimate ongoing surrender of the self through daily submission to God is the key that allows the real self, the real person, to emerge.

Many reading this book may have known God for years but may never have understood this principle. The spiritual life may not have grown within and developed as it should. Others may have known about God and believed in His existence, may even have acquired extensive theological training and understanding, without having enjoyed a rich spiritual life.

Understand the concept of repentance and all that can change. It is about seeing God with fresh eyes, with fresh truth by renewed vision. It is seeing with the heart not just the head.

Take it from me there can be no real change in our lives unless there is a change of mind. And that is what repentance is all about – changing our mind about where life is found.

Law 7

CULTIVATE YOUR SOUL

Cs

THE CULTIVATION OF THE SOUL

Everyone should know that you can't live in any other way
than by cultivating the soul. (Thomas Moore)[1]

A man was showing his friend around his beautiful garden on which he had lavished years of careful attention. Once it had been a wilderness with no shape or colour but years of hard work had turned it into a place of delight.

'This is indeed a beautiful garden,' the friend remarked. 'I don't think I have ever seen such order and loveliness. God most certainly is to be praised for such handiwork.'

The owner of the garden hesitated for a moment then said, 'Yes, God most certainly should be praised. But you should have seen it when He had it all to Himself!'

The truth is, of course, that like many things in this world success comes when God and man team up. Though God is the one who designed the soul, it requires care and husbandry on the part of the human being who possesses it, if it is to grow and develop in the way it should.

If the worship of God is the first law of the soul, then most certainly the cultivation of it is an important law also. If it isn't cultivated then it will degenerate and die!

Thousands of years ago King Solomon said this:

I went past the field of the sluggard,
  past the vineyard of the man who lacks judgment;
thorns had come up everywhere,
  the ground was covered with weeds,
  and the stone wall was in ruins.

*I applied my heart to what I observed
and learned a lesson from what I saw.*

Prov. 24:30–32

Those words could well describe the condition of someone who has neglected to cultivate their soul. Left to itself, without proper care and attention, the soul soon becomes like a garden overgrown with weeds.

This was the kind of thinking in the mind of Thomas Moore when he wrote his book *Care of the Soul.* Moore lived as a monk in a Catholic order for twelve years and therefore has a spiritual perspective to what he has to say. Later he trained as a psychotherapist and added a psychological dimension to his understanding.

John Bradshaw, another popular writer on the subject of soul care, said of Thomas Moore's book: 'From time to time I've been jolted by an extraordinary book which stops my world. It forces me to look at reality in a different way – a more expansive and meaningful way. It has provided a missing piece for me.'

Care of the Soul struck a national nerve and was on the *New York Times* hardcover bestseller list for eight months and has been acclaimed as one of the great books of the last decade of the twentieth century. Millions who read it were struck by the opening sentence of the book:

The greatest malady of the twentieth century, implicated in all our troubles and affecting us individually and socially is 'loss of soul'.[2]

When the soul is neglected, Moore pointed out, we experience all kinds of problems: obsessions, addictions, loss of meaning and emotional pain. By caring for our soul, he claimed, we can find relief from our distress and discover deep satisfaction and pleasure in life.

Although Moore 'has made the words *soul* and *soul care* very popular he defines them so broadly and vaguely,' says Gary Collins, a well-known evangelical writer and psychologist, 'that they mean almost nothing apart from one's intuition.' I agree.

WHAT IS THE SOUL?

Obviously the soul is not something tangible like a hand or a foot. It cannot be weighed, seen or analysed in a laboratory. My dictionary describes the soul as 'the non-physical aspect of a person in which is found the complex of human attributes that manifests as consciousness, thought, feeling and will'.

The word soul appears in Scripture about 130 times. The biblical writers didn't give it a precise technical definition. It appears, however, to bear the meaning of one's life and personality.

You can't really understand the soul; it is a mystery. People are sometimes referred to as experts in the affairs of the soul. I was introduced like this in one meeting and after thanking the chairman for his kind remarks pointed out that while I had some experience in the affairs of the soul I was not an expert.

There are not many soul doctors in the world today, says Lawrence Crabb. Plenty of psychologists, but not really people who know how to deal with the needs of the soul.

There may be experts in the realm of science, medicine, engineering – but not in the soul. It is not meant to be understood, but entered into. And it is immortal, says Scripture. Our soul will live on for ever in either hell or heaven, depending on our relationship to Jesus Christ.

As a counsellor I am often asked to deal with the soul and I wonder, as people open up their souls to me, whether they expect me, like a kind of mechanic, to take out some special psychological tool and fix them so that they can function again in the same old self-centred ways.

I have learned from my spiritual mentors that sometimes when one is counselling one has to speak for the soul. On one occasion a woman asked me to help her suppress her emotions because they were giving her so much trouble.

I decided to speak up for her soul. I said, 'Your soul is *meant* to feel. What we need to find out is what your emotions are telling you about your wrong goals and your wrong thinking. You cannot disown your soul without serious emotional consequences. Better to work with it than wish it were not there.'

When we turn to the Bible and ask ourselves the question, what is the soul? we get the best answers. Although there are many connotations to the word (and Bible writers didn't seem to give precise technical definitions to words like 'heart', 'mind' and 'soul'), the word appears to have two distinct meanings – life and personality.

When God created Adam he had life, as did the animals, but he was distinct from the animals – he was a person made in God's image (Gen. 1:27) with rational, volitional, emotional and spiritual characteristics. Think of the soul, then, as the core of your inner life and personality.

The soul in its highest sense is a vast capacity for God. I came across the following description of the soul many years ago. It is by Professor Henry Drummond and although it lacks technical definition, because of its sheer poetic beauty I go back to it and read it time and time again:

> The soul is like a curious chamber added on to being, and somehow involving being, a chamber with elastic and contractile walls, which can be expanded with God as its guest, illimitably but which without God shrinks and shrivels until every vestige of the Divine is gone and God's image is left without God's Spirit. One cannot call what is left a soul; it

is a shrunken useless organ, a capacity sentenced to death by a disease which drops as a withered hand by the side, and cumbers nature like a rotted branch. Life has its revenge upon neglect as well as upon extravagance. Misuse is as moral a sin as abuse.

C.S. Lewis had a similar thought in mind when he described the soul of a Christian as simply the hollow somewhere deep inside us which God fills.

There are three attitudes one can take toward the soul:

1. The soul is naturally Christian. (Tertullian, one of the Church Fathers was the first to propose this.)
2. The soul is naturally pagan.
3. The soul is naturally half pagan and half Christian.

I vote with Tertullian.

The soul (so I believe) is far from being naturally pagan. It is, in fact, *unnaturally* pagan – off centre, missing the way to live. When the soul opens itself to Christ then it has what Dr E. Stanley Jones calls 'a sense of homecoming upon it, of being reinstated, of being reconciled'.

Dr Jones tells of meeting a radiant man of eighty-two who said, 'I knew this was the Way, for the moment I put my feet upon it I was no longer fighting with myself.' That proved, said Dr Jones, that the way of Christ and the way of the soul were one.

If the soul were naturally pagan it would be uncomfortable coming into the kingdom, but the opposite is true; when it comes into the kingdom it has the feeling of coming into its own.

Again, if the soul were naturally pagan why should it be punished for its pagan ways? Surely it would be wrong to punish it for living according to its nature.

Do we not sense, even though we may sometimes suppress the feeling, that evil is evil and to be punished for it is just? In doing so do we not witness to our feeling that evil is unnatural?

C.S. Lewis, in *Screwtape Letters*, imagines a senior devil giving advice to a junior devil thus: 'We work under a cruel handicap. Nothing is naturally on our side. Everything has to be twisted before it is any use to us.'[3]

THE DISEASE OF THE SOUL

The soul fits into the kingdom of God like a hand fits into a glove. It was made by God and for God and will not reach its highest potential until it is at home with God. But our souls have been infected and afflicted with a disease call sin. What God formed, sin has deformed. That is the tragic doctrine of the Fall.

With that in mind we have to turn once again to the Scriptures which tell us that, as a result of Adam and Eve's transgression, the soul of everyone born in perpetuity contains a degenerative disease, which means that left to itself and without the salvation that comes through Jesus Christ, the soul will die.

The Bible is crystal clear on this point:

The soul who sins ... will die.

Ezek. 18:4

'Do not be afraid of those who kill the body but cannot kill the soul. Rather, be afraid of the One who can destroy both soul and body in hell.'

Matt. 10:28

For the wages of sin is death, but the gift of God is eternal life in Christ Jesus our Lord.

Rom. 6:23

THE LAW OF DEGENERATION

This principle of degeneration can be seen everywhere in nature. Plant a garden with roses and strawberries, leave it to itself for a few years and in process of time it will run to waste.

The law of degeneration runs through the whole of creation. If we neglect our body it will rapidly deteriorate. If it is the mind we neglect then it will degenerate into imbecility. If the conscience, it will run off into lawlessness and vice.

With this law or principle staring us in the face the words of the writer to the Hebrews rise almost to cosmic proportions:

For if the word spoken through angels proved steadfast, and every transgression and disobedience received a just reward, how shall we escape if we neglect so great a salvation, which at the first began to be spoken by the Lord, and was confirmed to us by those who heard Him.

Heb. 2:2, NKJV

If we neglect the usual means of keeping a garden in order how shall it escape turning to weeds? If we neglect the soul how shall it escape dissolution and death?

'Surely I was sinful at birth, sinful from the time my mother conceived me,' said the psalmist in Psalm 51:5. And experience shows that we will shape ourselves further into sin and ever deepening iniquity unless we expend some energy and effort to move against it.

Let me quote again from Professor Henry Drummond:

We are wont to imagine that Nature is full of life. In reality it is full of death. One cannot say it is natural for a plant to live. Examine its nature fully and you have to admit that its natural tendency is to die. It is kept from dying by a mere temporary endowment which gives it an ephemeral dominion over the elements – gives it power to utilise for a brief span, the rain, the sunshine and the air. Withdraw this temporary endowment for a moment and its true nature is revealed. Instead of overcoming nature it is overcome. The very things which appeared to minister to its growth and beauty now turn against it and make it decay and die. The sun which warmed it, withers it; the air and rain which nourished it, rots it.

It is the very forces which we associate with life which, when their true nature appears, are discovered to be really the ministers of death.[4]

When the Bible raises the question, 'How shall we escape if we neglect so great salvation?' you notice it does not answer it. It is a rhetorical question too obvious to need answering. In the very nature of things we cannot escape, any more than a man who has never learned to swim can escape drowning when he falls off a boat in the middle of the ocean.

If he has neglected to learn to swim and goes to sea, then he cannot complain if, when he is tossed overboard, he drowns. In the nature of things he cannot escape. Nor in the nature of things can the person who has neglected salvation.

What is this salvation which is spoken about here? It is more than just the mere forgiveness of sins (wonderful though that is) but the whole gamut of what God has done for us in Jesus Christ.

These words in Hebrews are being spoken to people who already had salvation in the sense of their sins having been forgiven. Salvation in its broadest sense is salvation from the downward bias of the soul. It takes in the whole process of rescue from the power of sin and selfishness that goes on all the time in our lives, the power that pulls us down, lowering us, blinding reason, searing conscience, paralysing the will.

THE ANTIDOTE

Now to counteract this law of degeneration God has introduced another law – the law of cultivation which will stop this downward drift in the soul and make it work the other way.

This is the active saving principle and fact of salvation. There is only one way to escape the problems that sin has introduced into the soul and that is to lay hold of God's salvation.

And as this salvation is the only power in the universe that can combat the principle of degeneration in the soul, how can we escape if we neglect it?

Is it not clear now why the Bible lays such emphasis upon a word that is so vital? It does not ask how we shall escape if we trample upon so great salvation, or doubt it or despise it, even. We have only to neglect it. A man who has been poisoned need only neglect the antidote in order to die. He does not need to dash it to the ground, pour it out of the window or rail against it. He will die whether he destroys it in a fit of passion or coolly refuses to have anything to do with it.

We need to keep in mind that the Christian life is a way of living and not merely a decision once made. In Acts we read:

Saul was still breathing out murderous threats against the Lord's disciples. He went to the high priest and asked him for letters to the synagogues in Damascus, so that if he found any there who belonged to the Way, whether men or women, he might take them as prisoners to Jerusalem.

Acts 9:1–2

About that time there arose a great disturbance about the Way.

Acts 19:23

Then Felix, who was well acquainted with the Way, adjourned the proceedings. 'When Lysias the commander comes,' he said, 'I will decide your case.'

Acts 24:22

The Way with a capital W is the way to do everything – to think, to feel, to act in every conceivable circumstance and in every relationship.

For centuries priests received into their charge the souls of those who lived within the boundaries of the church, called a parish. This responsibility of caring for the souls was known as *cura animarum*, the cure of souls.

Cure meant 'charge' as well as care. The parish priest was available at life's crucial moments, not as a doctor but simply to help the soul in times of birth, illness, crisis and death.

The role of the curate, as he was called, was to provide a spiritual context for the larger turning points in life. We can be the curators of our own souls and that idea implies an inner priesthood and a personal faith in God. And not only can we be the curators of our own souls – we should be. But we cannot do it on our own; we need the help of God. That means we must team up with the Almighty and open ourselves to the resources of the Holy Spirit if our souls are to develop and grow.

Many years ago I heard a preacher tell a story concerning a village organist who gave a recital on the chapel organ at a midweek gathering. This was in the days when large church organs would need someone to pump the wind into the instrument and usually they were positioned behind a curtain at the side of the organ.

After each item the organist would bow to the audience in acknowledgement of their applause and say, 'Now I will play the next piece which is …' and then he named it.

Returning to his stool after another bow he put his fingers on the keys but no sound came. He tried again and still there was no sound. After a moment or two the young boy whose task it was to pump air into the organ peered from behind the curtain and said, 'Let's have a little more "we" in it.'

So how do we go about the task of cultivating the soul? How do we avoid the loss of soul that Thomas Moore talks about?

TIME WITH THE LORD

It begins, I believe, by getting alone with God in a daily quiet time in which we talk to Him in prayer, read and meditate on His Word, listen to His voice and give ourselves in obedience to everything He reveals to us.

The soul is renewed in daily contact with God. Neglect this and the result will be emptiness of the soul. The soul needs time with God if it is to develop and grow. Those Christians who say they are too busy to spend time with God in prayer and meditation will find that this neglect of the soul will have serious repercussions in their lives.

Steven Covey tells the story of a man who was trying to cut a log with a saw that needed sharpening. When this was pointed out to him the man replied, 'I haven't time to sharpen the saw. To stop now means I won't get through this log in time.'

If you are too busy to spend time with God and refresh your soul then you are far busier than you ought to be. The great reformer Martin Luther used to say, 'I have so much to do today I'll need to spend another hour on my knees.'

James Russell Lowell says:

If the chosen soul could never be alone
In deep mid silence, open-doored to God,
No greatness ever had been dreamed or done.
The nurse of full-grown souls is solitude.

One of the things that saddens me about the contemporary Christian scene is this lack of emphasis on the need to spend time daily alone with God.

That regular daily spiritual tête-à-tête with God which was the habit of Christians in times past now appears to have been abandoned by many modern-day Christians – though thankfully not all.

When I raised my concern about this with a group of younger Christians some time ago I was told, 'Times are changing. People are much busier now than they used to be. Anyway, it's possible to have a perpetual quiet time in your soul no matter where you are. The lines to heaven are always open, not just between 6.30 and 7.30 in the morning.'

And there was one other objection: 'Legalism is what drove many Christians in times past to keep slavishly to the morning quiet time. In days gone by people said a quick prayer and read their Bibles because they felt if they did not give God fifteen minutes at the beginning of the day He might push them under a bus or something. We are more real nowadays and free of this type of legalism. We are free to be ourselves.'

There is no doubt that over the years many Christians have come to the daily quiet time constrained only by a sense of duty. They read a passage from the Bible, say a quick prayer and then, glad that duty has been done, turn with eagerness to other things, the newspaper, perhaps, or the events of the day.

For many the duty very rarely became a delight. Call it legalism or whatever you will, but that is not how a quiet time ought to be – or needs to be. It has certainly not been like that in my experience.

Honesty compels me to admit that my personal quiet times have not always been spiritually exciting and exhilarating. On occasions I have hit some hard patches and gone through a number of dry and arid spiritual experiences, but all in all I have to say that the greatest catalyst in my growth as a Christian has been those times when I have met with the Lord devotionally.

For years now, a conviction has been growing in my heart that the Christian life rises and falls at the point of the devotional – those times when one meets privately with the Lord to deepen one's intimacy with Him. There the soul becomes at its best.

Is it possible to have a perpetual quiet time in your soul no matter where you are? Of course it is. No one had a more perpetual quiet time in His soul than Jesus, but over and over again in the Gospels we read how He would get up early, before the crack of dawn, to be alone with God and pray.

But can't we pray as the Bible tells us to – at all times? Why do we need stated times for prayer? As a young and impetuous youth I remember speaking up in a Bible class on one occasion when we were studying the text in Ephesians 6:18: 'Pray in the Spirit on all occasions with all kinds of prayers.' I wanted to make the revolutionary point that if this verse was true then prayer meetings were unnecessary – we should cancel them in favour of always praying in our hearts.

The leader of the Bible class replied wisely: 'If you are to pray always there must be specific times for the cultivation of such a spirit of continuous prayer. You cannot pray everywhere,' he said, 'unless you first learn to pray somewhere. You cannot maintain the spirit of prayer unless you make a specific time or times for prayer.' I came away convinced.

But what about the argument that people are busier now than they used to be and that it is impossible in today's busy world to maintain a daily quiet time? The fact that we are busier than we used to be is no argument for cutting down or cutting out a daily quiet time. It is rather an argument for re-prioritising. If we are to have enough spiritual resources and to spare, then we must be sure to provide for replenishing those resources. This is done in the quiet time. Quite frankly, if you are too busy to have a quiet time then you are busier than God intends you to be.

As Dr E. Stanley Jones says,

A diver who would be too busy to think about making sure his air supply is in good working order before he descends into the depths would be no more foolish than the man who descends into the stifling atmosphere of today's world without getting his breathing apparatus of prayer connected with the pure air of the kingdom of God.[5]

If we grow spiritually anaemic and pale it is because we have done ourselves this harm – the harm of self-inflicted asphyxiation.

A poet wrote:

What a frail soul he gave me,
And a heart lame and unlikely
for the large events.

I wonder whether we don't give ourselves 'a heart lame and unlikely for the large events' when we abandon the infinite resources God has given us for the asking and the taking.

The quiet time is where the soul grows receptive, where prayer becomes the organ of spiritual touch which in turn becomes as healing and as effective as the touch of the woman upon the hem of Christ's garment (Luke 8:40–48).

The great French writer Blaise Pascal once declared, 'Nearly all the ills of life spring from this simple source – that we are not able to sit still in a room.' But what if in that stillness we would meet with God? How healing and resourceful that would be.

If due to circumstances the quiet time cannot be established on a *daily* basis, then make it on as *regular* a basis as possible. There are times in my own life when, through sickness, travelling or some emergency, I am not able to have a daily quiet time; but I return to the daily habit as quickly as I can. I now count every day ill-spent which does not include some time given to prayer and the reading of God's Word.

HOW DO WE DO IT?

Convinced of the need for a daily quiet time, how should we go about establishing it? Different temperaments will prefer different approaches. Some might like to sit outside and admire the creation; others prefer settling down in a private room and meditating against a background of Christian music. Whatever the context there are certain essentials we must adopt if we are to maximise the quiet time and make it contribute to spiritual growth.

First, decide on the amount of time you can give to it and draw a fence around that period. Ideally this should be at least fifteen minutes.

More is better. Guard your privacy as much as possible, shutting yourself in a room, distancing yourself from the telephone and so on.

If the pattern of your life does not allow for a quiet time then *make time*. Go over your days in the presence of God and see what you can cut out. It may be necessary to treat some things with what someone has called 'studied neglect'.

You must not neglect anything essential, like time with your family, for example, but I think you will find, as thousands have done over the centuries, that when you make it your chief concern to establish a daily appointment with God you will be amazed at how He will help you recast your priorities.

There is no doubt that the first part of the morning is best for this, though of course for some this is not always possible. Why the morning? The morning is when the soul is alert, looking out to the day, when it is filled with a sense of expectancy. Time spent with God in the morning helps tune the soul for what lies ahead.

Another unknown poet put it like this:

Every morning lean thine arm awhile
Upon the window sill of heaven
And gaze upon thy God.
Then with the vision in thy heart
Turn strong to meet the day.

C.S. Lewis had this to say about the morning:

The real problem of the Christian life comes … the very moment you wake up each morning. All your wishes and hopes for the day rush at you like wild animals. And the first job each morning consists in shoving them all back; in listening to that other voice, taking that other view, letting that other, larger, stronger, quieter life come flowing in.[6]

Whenever possible use the same room or spot. It gathers associations over time and this you will find helps greatly.

READ YOUR BIBLE

The Bible, I believe, should always be at the centre of your quiet time. So begin by taking your Bible and reading a portion of it. George Muller, the famous Christian who founded the Bristol orphanages, said that the greatest spiritual discovery he had ever made was the effectiveness of reading a passage from the Bible before getting down to prayer. 'Prior to that,' he said, 'the prayer time was not easy for me, but I discovered that reading the Scriptures before I prayed helped prime the spiritual pump and made my prayer times so much more powerful.'

Don't be tempted, as many are nowadays, to skip the reading of the Bible in your quiet time. Research shows that people in general are not reading as much as they used to. It's part of this thing called postmodernism that lays more emphasis on the emotional than the rational, more on experiences and feelings than on objective truth.

Bulky books, say publishers, are going out of fashion. People today have neither the time nor the inclination to read them. Thin paperbacks are the order of the day and there is a lot of literary slimming going on.

Sadly, this cultural phenomenon is being reflected in the Christian Church. The Bible, however, is a bulky book. Don't develop a fondness for the *Reader's Digest Condensed Version* of the Scriptures, which in my opinion is one of the most foolish versions ever attempted.

Every word of Scripture is important. 'All Scripture,' said Paul when writing to Timothy, 'is God-breathed and is useful for teaching, rebuking, correcting and training in righteousness, so that the man of God may be thoroughly equipped for every good work' (2 Tim. 3:16).

I know a woman who has a non-Christian husband. After she became a Christian she began to read her Bible every day and after a number of months her husband, seeing her dipping daily into her Bible, said, 'Haven't you finished that book yet?'

The Bible is a book we will never finish, for every time we open it God has something fresh to say to us from its pages. He who spoke into it speaks through it still.

The Bible, it must be remembered, is God's one and only published work. As one preacher put it, 'The Bible is in a category all by itself. It is not the first of a group; it is in a classification alone. It is not the leader of equals; it is a book apart.'

Whatever degree of inspiration we may attach to other Christian writings (*The Pilgrim's Progress*, for example), the Bible is unique in that it is the only book that contains the record of our Lord's incarnate life, the spiritual pilgrimage of the race out of which He came, and the birth of the Christian Church.

That being so, we ought to reverence it, respect it, store our memory with precious fragments of it, learn its highways and byways and make the reverent reading of it a privileged part of every day.

If you don't know how to read the Bible, join one of the many Bible reading organisations that distribute Bible notes. At comparatively small cost they provide selected passages and notes.

Before you read a passage from the Bible offer a brief prayer for understanding. The prayer I use whenever I open my Bible to read it is the one used by the psalmist: 'Open my eyes that I may see wonderful things in your law' (Psa. 119:18).

Read the Bible slowly, letting the words soak in. If some verse strikes you, let your mind circle around it in a few moments of meditation; it will render up new meanings to you. Write those thoughts in a notebook or in the margin of your Bible.

Another issue that is not being emphasised in today's Christian society is the importance of meditating on a word or sentence or thought taken from Scripture.

'Great matters,' said one philosopher, 'have to be given a second thought.' That is precisely what meditation is – giving a biblical word or text a second thought. There is no time or space to go into the practice of meditation here, but let me encourage you to read what I have written on this subject in *Getting the Best out of the Bible – the Art of Meditation*.[7]

I promise you that once you have grasped the concept of Bible meditation and put it into practice, this is what will happen: you will find your soul becoming the workshop of an unseen Sculptor who will chisel in the secret chambers of your soul the living forms that constitute a deeper knowledge of Him. As a result your spiritual life will become richer and more wonderful than you could ever imagine.

After your reading, relax and say, 'Father, have you anything to say to me?' Begin to listen. Become guidable. Of course some are sceptical that God speaks directly to His children and would view it as impertinence to suggest that He should do so. Someone has said, 'If you talk to God that is prayer; if He talks to you that is schizophrenia.'

At first you may hear nothing, but gradually over time you will learn to disentangle the voice of God from all the other voices – the whisperings of the subconscious, the clamour of personal ambition, the murmur of self-will and so on.

LISTEN TO GOD

The art of listening to the voice of the Spirit in prayer has also been strangely neglected. But those who have practised this quiet waiting upon Him tell us that a trained ear comes to recognise the voice of the Spirit and knows when He has spoken.

Note the phrase 'a trained ear'. I have talked to many Christians who have told me: 'The listening side of prayer baffles me. I sit still and listen, but all I hear are the sounds in the distance, the traffic, the barking of a dog, an aeroplane flying overhead, perhaps. It just doesn't seem to work for me.'

Listening to God is an art. It is not learned in a single session. The following words taken from *Creative Prayer* by Mrs Herman helped me greatly:

> *The soul that waits in silence must learn to disentangle the voice of God from the net of other voices – the ghostly whisperings of the subconscious, the luring voices of the world, the hindering voices of misguided friendship, the clamour of personal ambition and vanity, the murmur of self-will, the song of unbridled imagination, the thrilling note of religious romance. To learn to keep one's ear true in so subtle a labyrinth of spiritual sound is indeed at once a great adventure and education. One hour of such listening may give us a deeper insight ... and surer instinct for divine values than a year's hard study.*[8]

The listening side of prayer does not come easily. It costs in terms of time but the rewards are worth far more than it costs. It took me well over six months to learn to quiet my soul and cultivate the art of listening to God's voice. I would sit sometimes for half-an-hour or so and hear nothing. But gradually I learned, as Mrs Herman put it, how to 'disentangle the voice of God from the net of other voices'.

As exercise strengthens the body and education enlarges the mind, so our sensitivity to God develops and grows as we learn to wait in silence before Him.

What does God's voice sound like? That is a question that has often been put to me. Different people have different experiences. To some God's voice comes in the form of a gentle impression. To others a verse of Scripture takes on a special power as God speaks directly to the heart. Sometimes one is conscious of one's own thoughts being accompanied by such a sense of the divine presence that one is convinced God is thinking through you.

One thing, however, must be said in relation to the listening side of prayer. Those who would cultivate the power to know His voice must set time aside specifically for it and set it aside every day.

Jesus said, 'My sheep listen to my voice; I know them, and they follow me' (John 10:27). He wants to speak with us; do we want to listen to Him?

PRAY

Finally, say to God what you have to say. In other words talk to Him about whatever is on your heart. This we generally refer to as 'prayer'. Always begin by thanking Him and praising Him for His goodness. Our Lord, you remember, said in answer to His disciples' plea, 'Teach us to pray', 'This, then, is how you should pray, "Our Father in heaven, hallowed be your name ..."' (Luke 11:1; Matt. 5:9). '*Hallowed be your name.*' Note that. Prayer should always begin by hallowing His name; in other words, worshipping Him for what He does and for who He is.

At times you may feel an intense desire to pray for the needs of others – friends, family, loved ones or even acquaintances who are ill or in distress. This we call intercession.

Prayer must not become self-centred, praying only for the things that interest you. The following prayer was found among the papers of a Member of Parliament who died a couple of centuries ago. It is not known whether it was his prayer or someone else's but it is a perfect example of how not to pray.

O Lord, Thou knowest I have mine estates in the City of London and likewise that I have lately purchased an estate in the County of Essex. I beseech Thee to preserve the two counties of Middlesex and Essex from fire and earthquake, and as I have a mortgage in Hereford I beg Thee likewise to have an eye of compassion on that county. For the rest of the counties Thou mayest deal with them as Thou art pleased.[9]

Always remember to thank Him for the answers He gives to your prayers. God *always* answers. Sometimes He says yes, other times no. No is an answer as well as yes – sometimes a better answer. Other times He will say wait, I will give you something better. But He always answers. One preacher put it like this:

If the request isn't right He answers 'No'.
If the timing isn't right He answers 'Slow'.
If you aren't ready yet His answer is 'Grow'.
If everything is right and ready His answer is 'Go'.

A traveller tells how he stood on board a ship as it entered one of the locks of the Panama Canal. He writes:

> *The great sea gates were closed upon us. We who had sailed the oceans were blocked, shut in, helpless, our freedom gone. But lo, we felt a great lifting, great fountains were opened from beneath and to our astonishment, that great ship was lifted thirty-five feet in just seven minutes. Then the gates opened and we glided out on a higher level on to the bosom of Lake Gatun.*

The quiet time does that – it shuts you in with God, the door closes upon you and then infinite resources begin to bubble up from beneath and you are lifted up. The door opens and you glide out onto a higher level of life. You will be surprised – and other people will too – at how easily you transcend worries and fears and difficulties and seem to live life on a higher level. It's the result of being shut in with God.

That's the power of the quiet time – the place where the soul grows best.

Notes

Preface

1.   Mark Buchanan, *Your God is Too Safe* (Oregon: Multnomah Publishers, 2001).

Introduction: 'You'd Better Change Course'

1.   Henry Drummond, *Natural Law in the Spiritual World* (Society of Metaphysicians, 1998).

2.   E. Stanley Jones, *The Way* (London: Hodder & Stoughton, 1947).

3.   Luci Shaw, quoted by Edward England in *The Addiction of a Busy Life* (Crowborough, Aviemore Books, 1998).

4.   Stephen R. Covey, *The 7 Habits of Highly Effective People* (London: Simon and Schuster, 1989).

5.   Malcolm Muggeridge, *A 20th Century Testimony* (Nashville, TN: Thomas Nelson, 1978).

Law Number 1: First Things First

1.   Foreword to Ronald Barclay Allen, *Praise! A Matter of Life and Breath* (Nashville, TN: Thomas Nelson, 1980).

2.   C.S. Lewis, *Reflections in the Psalms* (London: Fontana, HarperCollins, 1960).

3.   Harold S. Kushner, *When Bad Things Happen to Good People* (London: Pan, 2000).

4.   C.S. Lewis, *The Lion, the Witch and the Wardrobe* (Middlesex: Penguin, 1959).

5.   Eugene Peterson, *Living The Message* (London: HarperCollins, 1996).

Law Number 2: Count Your Blessings

1.   Reported in *Ten Golden Rules for Financial Success* by Gary Moore (Grand Rapids: Zondervan Publishing House, 1996) p.38.

2.   Dr W.E. Sangster, *Westminster Sermons* (London: Epworth Press, 1961).

Law Number 3: Keeping On Keeping On

1.   John R.W. Stott, *The Contemporary Christian* (Leicester: InterVarsity Press, 1992) p.161.

2.   Dr Scott Peck, *The Road Less Travelled* (London: Arrow, 1990).

3. Os Guinness, *Doubt* (Oxford: Lion Publishing, 1976).

4. Taken from *The Encyclopaedia of Christian Quotations*, compiled by Mark Water (Alresford: John Hunt Publishing, 2000).

5. Os Guinness, *The Call* (Milton Keynes: Word Publishing, 1998).

Law Number 4: Remember to Forget

1. Amy Carmichael, *If* (London: Triangle, 1987).

Law Number 5: Give Yourself to Others

1. Quoted in *The 7 Habits of Highly Effective People* by Stephen R. Covey (London: Simon and Schuster, 1989).

2. Thomas S. Kuhn, *The Structure of Scientific Revolutions* (Chicago: University of Chicago Press, 1996).

3. D. Broughton Knox, *The Everlasting God* (Darlington, Co Durham: Evangelical Press, 1982).

4. Eugene Peterson, *Living The Message* (London: HarperCollins, 1996) p.25.

5. J.B. Phillips, *When God was Man* (Nashville, TN: Abingdon Press, 1955).

Law Number 6: Stay Close to God

1. Charles W. Colson, *Born Again* (London: Hodder & Stoughton, 1979).

2. Ibid.

3. Charles W. Colson, *Against the Night* (Bournemouth: Vine Books, 1999).

4. John White, *Changing on the Inside* (Guildford: Eagle, 1991).

5. Ibid.

6. Charles W. Colson, *Born Again*, op. cit.

7. C.S. Lewis, *Perelandra* (London: Harper Collins, 2000).

Law Number 7: Cultivate Your Soul

1. Thomas Moore, *Care of the Soul* (London: Piatkus Books, 1992).

2. Ibid.

3. C.S. Lewis, *The Screwtape Letters* (London: Fount, 1988).

4. Henry Drummond, *Natural Law in the Spiritual World* (Society of Metaphysicians, 1998).

5. E. Stanley Jones, *The Way* (London: Hodder & Stoughton, 1947).

6. C.S. Lewis, *Mere Christianity* (London: Fount, 1997).

7.   Selwyn Hughes, *Getting the Best out of the Bible – the Art of Meditation* (Farnham: CWR, 1989).

8.   Mrs E. Herman, *Creative Prayer* (R.A. Kessinger Publishing Co., 1998).

9.   From *The Pure in Heart*, Dr W.E. Sangster (London: Epworth Press, 1954).

Applying the
7 Laws
OF SPIRITUAL SUCCESS

**WORKBOOK FOR PERSONAL
OR GROUP APPLICATION**

Jennifer Oldroyd

Foreword

'No matter how powerful and effective the ointment,' said an ancient philosopher, 'it is of little use unless it is applied to the affected part.' It is the same with truth; its power lies not just in the insight it brings but also in its application.

Application is the theme of this workbook and study guide written by Jennifer Oldroyd. She has set out to help you relate the concepts contained in *7 Laws of Spiritual Success* to your daily spiritual life and experience. You will see also that she has brought some further insights into the topics discussed which will help expand your understanding of these important biblical concepts.

I wish to record my thanks and appreciation for the time and effort she has put into making *7 Laws of Spiritual Success* more readily accessible for those who wish to pursue them either as a personal study or in company with others.

The key to getting the best out of this study guide is to begin by reading through the Preface. This provides you with recommendations on how to use this book. I can't stress enough how important it is to do this.

My prayer is that this study guide will not only clarify the concepts contained in *7 Laws of Spiritual Success*, but will help you to apply them to your life in a way that will deepen your walk with the Lord and enable you to become an even bigger and better channel through whom Christ's love can flow to others.

My love in the Lord Jesus
Selwyn Hughes, 2004

Preface

This workbook has been produced to help you make the most of *7 Laws of Spiritual Success*. Selwyn Hughes distilled fifty years of teaching and ministry into what he believed is an irreducible minimum of just seven elements. To spend time studying these elements will be like a spiritual health check. It will enable you to measure your priorities and your heart condition, and to make a diagnosis with the help of the Holy Spirit.

You would consult a doctor about symptoms that trouble you, or a nutritionist about problems with your weight, or an optician about failing eyesight. What do you do when spiritual problems confront you? When prayer is difficult, worship feels dull and lifeless, when the Scriptures themselves are dry and unappetising?

One thing you can do is to turn back the pages of your Christian experience, and look once again at those basic premises which once seemed so life-changing. Maybe you have become unforgiving to someone. Maybe you have lost the habit of gratitude to God for His many blessings. Maybe you have given up trying so hard.

As you open your mind and heart to these first principles, it may be that you will need to make some changes; to repent and turn from some wrong attitudes. The probing questions and practical Action Plan in each chapter will help you do just that.

HOW TO USE THIS BOOK

1. You will need to have read right through *7 Laws of Spiritual Success* at least once, but preferably twice.

2. Decide how much time you want to spend on each chapter. If you are studying alone, you may want to do, say, 15 minutes a day, taking one section at a time. If you are studying as a group, then you might want to spend one or two sessions on each chapter.

3. Each section of the workbook contains questions to help you think through and apply what you have learned. Space has been left on the pages for you to note down answers to the questions, but a separate notebook would enable you to make more extensive notes, including prayers, thoughts and specific courses of action. The more practical your response, the more you are likely to see God at work in your life.

4. At the end of each chapter you will find an Action Plan. This consists of suggestions, questions and ideas for putting into practice the lessons learned. Even if you are using this book for personal and private study, it would be good to share this section with one or two others. Agreeing together on specific courses of action will strengthen your resolve, empower your prayers and offer a better chance of actually making changes in your life and the life of your church.

5. The aim of this book is to direct your thoughts and attention to Scripture. Refer constantly to your Bible throughout. Check all the references, and read the verses before and after the selected portions. And each time you begin to study, ask the Holy Spirit to guide, challenge and inspire you.

Most courses of study finish with an examination to discover what you have learned and how well you understand it. Here you will find no such test. There are plenty of questions, but no 'right' answers. The exam you will take will be the daily one of living out the purposes of God, making His kingdom come and His will done in your sphere of life. You will receive no diploma, but if you truly try to live your life according to the laws of God, you will one day receive a crown, and hear His voice saying, 'Well done, good and faithful servant!'

Introduction

'YOU'D BETTER CHANGE COURSE'

"A book that helped me more than any other was

Professor Henry Drummond's Natural Law in the

Spiritual World ... *as I sought to understand the concept*

of laws being present not only in the natural world but

also in the spiritual world ...

As I pondered this issue I tried to imagine a

universe where everything happened not by law

but by chance ..." (p.3)

NATURAL LAWS

The first chapter of Genesis introduces us to the Creator God. A child reading this account of the beginning of our world might say, 'God made the sun. God made the birds. God made the flowers. God made me.' The child would be right, but would only have brushed the surface of what Genesis is telling us about the Creator.

Dig a little deeper into those verses and you will find that what God was doing was not only bringing the physical world into being, but also anchoring it to His will with immutable laws. Not only did He say, 'Let there be light', He also decided how fast it would travel, and established the laws of reflection and refraction. Not only did He create the sun and the stars, He also established their orbits, and the rhythm that governs our lives: the mornings and evenings, the days and the weeks, the months and the years.

And this is the same God who rules over the spiritual realm.

Those who are art critics can often name the artist of any painting instantly. They recognise the brush work, the use of light and shade, the way in which paint is applied. In the same way, we can recognise the hand of God. '*The great lines running through the universe which we call "laws" do not stop at what scientists call "the natural sphere", but are to be observed in the spiritual sphere also*' (p.2). In the pages that follow, Selwyn Hughes demonstrates that there are laws which govern the spiritual world, recognising in their design and immutability the same Artist who created the wonderful universe in which we live.

Questions to consider

- 'The idea was quite new to me' (p.2). Is this idea new to you? What is your initial response?

_____

_____

_____

_____

- Selwyn Hughes' guest was 'a young scientist' (p.2). Do you think that might have coloured the way he thought?

_____

_____

_____

_____

SPIRITUAL LAWS

When men and women make laws, they often have to change them in order to reflect the changes in society. For example, in Britain the licensing laws have changed, and lots of pubs and bars now stay open all day. And it is no longer against the law to have a homosexual relationship.

This happens in the Church also. The Anglican Church has changed the law on women in the priesthood. And they are considering changing the law on remarriage of divorced persons.

For us, laws are tools that we use to govern society, to make our citizens feel safe and protected, and to provide a pattern for living that will be the best for the majority. And when we think the tool has become 'outdated', we scrap it.

However, in this next section of his Introduction, Selwyn Hughes introduces the idea that the spiritual laws which the Creator God has established are *'as sure, certain and reliable as those we have discovered in the natural realm'* (p.4). This is the idea that we are going to have to accept before we go any further in this book. If it is true, then the principles of worship, forgiveness, perseverance, and so on, are not optional extras. They are not laws that operated in the eighteenth or nineteenth or twentieth century, but not in the twenty-first. 'Obey and you get results; disobey and you get consequences' (p.9). This is as true for us as it was for Adam.

Questions to consider

- Does the thought of immutable spiritual laws make you feel secure or threatened? (See the lighthouse story on p.11!)

- '*It is impossible for us to break laws; we only break ourselves upon them*' (Cecil B. De Mille, p.11). Have you ever experienced this? What happened?

TRUE SUCCESS

What did you think when you first saw the title of this book? There are probably Christians who would be offended by each part of the title. Only *seven* laws? But we are not under *law* any more! And, of course, surely it's wrong to talk of spiritual *success*?

The dictionary gives a number of definitions of the word success: 'good fortune; prosperous progress or achievement; the attainment of wealth, influence or acclaim'. As those who want to follow the carpenter of Nazareth, we would want to repudiate some of these concepts.

But, as Selwyn Hughes shows, the idea of progress or achievement is not an unbiblical one and nor, actually, is the idea of prosperity – not the prosperity of 'wealth, influence or acclaim', but that of '*soul prosperity*' (p.13).

*Does the Bible use the concept of success? Most definitely.
The word 'success' and its synonyms, appear many times in
Scripture. Here are just a few:*

> *Do not let this Book of the Law depart from your mouth;
> meditate on it day and night, so that you may be careful to
> do everything written in it. Then you will be prosperous and
> successful.*
>
>

Josh. 1:8

> *He [Uzziah] sought God during the days of Zechariah, who
> instructed him in the fear of God. As long as he sought the
> LORD, God gave him success.*
>
>

2 Chron. 26:5

> *So he sent David away from him and gave him command over
> a thousand men, and David led the troops in their campaigns.
> In everything he did he had great success, because the LORD
> was with him.*
>
>

1 Sam. 18:13–14

*What did God have in mind when He said He would give His
servants success? It meant of course that God would bless the work
of their hands, but God had in mind soul prosperity, too. (p.13)*

If we are honest, we do want to make progress with God. We
want to learn more about Him, to understand more of His Word, to
serve Him better. That, for us, would be success. If we want success

in the garden, the farm or the laboratory, we have to work within the natural laws. And if we want success in the spiritual life, then we have to recognise the laws that operate there too.

Questions to consider

- *'Success in a Christian sense is this: knowing the will of God and doing it'* (p.14). On this basis, would you say you are making a success of your spiritual life?

- *'No one can be truly successful if he or she is not a person of character'* (p.14). Who is the most spiritually 'successful' person you know? Does his or her life and character bear this statement out?

ACTION PLAN

- *'The law of the Spirit of life, the controlling power of the Holy Spirit – who is life-giving – is stronger in the believer than the controlling power of sin which ultimately produces death'* (p.5). Spend some time asking the Holy Spirit to use the study of this book to lead you into the truth.

- Look up the word 'success' in a concordance, and note how often in Scripture God promises it, and grants it, to those who are truly searching for Him and trying to obey Him.

- Make a list of the areas of your Christian life that you feel are the weakest, and ask God to use this book to reveal where you are going wrong. Keep a record of the answers!

- Selwyn Hughes used the concept of spiritual laws in this book in his work as a pastor and counsellor. Think about what areas of your life it could impact: your job, raising your children, teaching Sunday school, caring for elderly relatives, and so on.

- Ask God to plant the principle of this book in your mind as an *'"apperception thought" … a powerful notion or idea that establishes itself in your mind and around which other similar ideas and thoughts easily encrust'* (p.6), and to speak to you in lots of different ways as you work through the study.

Law 1

FIRST THINGS FIRST

"The first responsibility of every Christian is to worship

God. It is, I believe, the first law of the soul.

When we violate that law we put our souls

in peril" (p.21)

MAKE WORSHIP YOUR FIRST FOCUS

In recent years there has been a spate of TV programmes and newspaper articles devoted to 'lists': the top 100 people, or books, or programmes. Even if we find our personal favourite down at number 75, we still want to know what made 'Number One'.

As you start this journey with Selwyn Hughes, this spiritual check-up, are you surprised by his 'Number One'? What did you think it would be? What would you have voted for? What one element of the Christian faith and journey would *you* have put at the top?

Selwyn Hughes has drawn on his experiences in churches, fellowships and in the counselling room, to highlight that when we fail to put the worship of God first in our hearts and minds, in our thinking and planning, in our work and witness, we fail to become what God created us to be.

Many organisations now require their employees to keep a record of how they spend their time at work. Our perception of what we do all day can often differ greatly from the reality. Making a note of every action and how long it took can soon throw up answers to the question, 'Where did the time go?'

So, too, for us as Christians. We may think that we give generously – but do we keep a careful record? We may think that we are living a life of prayer – but how much time is actually spent in prayer? And we may believe that the worship of God is a clear priority, but even a quick 'stock take' may reveal that this is not so. We may indeed spend time on Sunday worshipping God with our friends and family, but as Selwyn Hughes says:

> *… it is not so much with corporate worship I am concerned here; rather it is with individual worship. I am thinking of it in the way that Jesus used the word when tempted by the devil in the wilderness.* (p.20)

Questions to consider

• Is the worship of God a missing element in your life, or in the life of your church (p.18)?

• On p.23 Selwyn says, '*God meant that every convert should learn first how to worship Him and only after that become a worker.*' Was that your experience as a new Christian? How were you taught about worship?

- Read Genesis 22:1–14 and Job 1. How do these stories change your view of what worship is?

WORSHIP AND OUR UNDERSTANDING OF GOD

Sunday schools are a rich source of funny stories about children's misunderstandings. There was the child who thought the song said that God would make us 'vicious old men', rather than 'fishers of men'. Or the little boy who prayed, 'Our Father, who art in heaven, Harold be thy name …'

Inexperience and immaturity may result in misunderstanding. If not sorted out, misunderstanding may lead to wrong beliefs, and wrong beliefs may lead to all kinds of problems in our emotional and spiritual lives.

On pages 28–35, Selwyn Hughes explores some of these problems, and shows the importance of trusting God, and also having a true and right concept of God.

If you are a self-taught tennis player or golfer, you may have had to resort to proper instruction to take you forward in your game. And you may have found that some bad techniques have had to be 'unlearned'. Similarly, whether you have been a Christian a long time, or just a few years, there may be some ideas and beliefs that you have absorbed that will have to be discarded.

On page 32 is the story of Dr Joseph Cooke, who '*invented an impossible God*'. It may be that your own background and upbringing have left you with an understanding of God that is false. Your parents' beliefs, your experiences as a child or young person, unhappy situations with other Christians – these may all have shaped your view of God. And, as Selwyn Hughes explains, it is your view of God that determines your worship.

The good news, however, is that the work of the Holy Spirit is to lead us into all truth (John 16:13). Ask Him to show you whether there is any misunderstanding or wrong view of God in your life, and to teach you how to worship in spirit and in truth.

Questions to consider

- Has anything happened in your life that has made it difficult for you to trust God (p.30)?

- How do you feel about the quote from *The Lion, the Witch and the Wardrobe* on page 33 about God not being 'safe'?

....

....

....

....

WORSHIP AND WORK

Every time a sermon is given on the story of Mary and Martha, there will be some dear lady in the congregation who will go out of church muttering, 'That's all very well, but *someone* has to cook the dinner.'

The Protestant work ethic is alive and well and living in many Christian homes and workplaces and churches. The busier we are, the more we think we are serving God and pleasing Him. Meetings and committees, youth work and evangelism, services and celebrations, catering and counselling – we fill our time with the things we do for God. The thought of Mary, sitting smugly and comfortably at Jesus' feet, secretly annoys us, and if we end up burnt out and close to a nervous breakdown, we see it as an acceptable sacrifice to God.

This last section of Selwyn Hughes' chapter underlines for us that those who serve best are actually those who serve as a consequence of their worship of God.

So what does that mean in practice? Must I join a contemplative order? Must I rise at 5am every day to worship God before I do anything else? Must I give up all my 'Christian work' until I've got the balance right?

Selwyn Hughes suggests reading Matthew 11:28–29 in *The Message*, and meditating on that lovely phrase 'the rhythms of grace'. The whole created world has a rhythm: day and night, work and rest, times of growth and times of dormancy. By putting the worship of God first in our lives, we will more easily 'find the rhythm'.

Questions to consider

- Oswald Chambers says, '*The biggest competitor for devotion is service*' (p.37). Do you think that Christian work has a right place in your life, or has it become a greater priority than worship?

- Do you identify with the quote from Eugene Peterson on page 38: '*Without worship we live manipulated and manipulating lives*'? Do you feel that events in your life have 'manipulated' you?

ACTION PLAN

- '*We hardly know where to begin because we have lost nearly all contact with the past*' (Robert Webber, p.19). Write down now some ideas of how you could begin to give the worship of God its rightful place in your life and the life of your church.

- '*One of the failures of modern-day Christians is to put work before worship. We take our converts and immediately set about making workers out of them. God never meant it to be so*' (p.23). What plans could your church make to ensure that new Christians are taught correctly about the primacy of worship?

- '*Most problems arise in the personality as a result of our failure truly to worship God*' (Larry Crabb, p.29). Are there problems in your life or in the life of your church? Start to look at those problems in the light of this chapter: how might your problems be connected with your attitude to the worship of God? How can you begin to change things?

- '*I urge you, before you go any further, to think through this issue of how you see God, for if you do not see Him as He really is – trustworthy, reliable and good – then those doubts and misgivings will sabotage true worship*' (p.33). Sit down with another person and take it in turns to describe God to each other. What are the words and phrases you each use, and what do they tell you about your perception of God? How might you develop your view of God?

- *'When I meet a Christian leader I meet a manager'* (Os Guinness, p.37). How can your church encourage its leaders to get the balance right between work and worship?

Law 2

COUNT YOUR BLESSINGS

Cb

"It is another law of life, I believe, that the more we dwell

on what we have, rather than what we don't have, the more

the personality is drawn to health" (p.42)

FOCUS ON YOUR BLESSINGS

The first story in this chapter is about someone who regularly, first thing in the morning, lists five new things that God has done for him. But have you ever noticed how easy it is to build up a list of negative things?

It may be that some really bad thing happens to us. Perhaps redundancy, or cancer, or bereavement. We start to learn to deal with it. But then something else happens. Something much smaller, but still bad – maybe a back problem, or a financial setback. Somehow, it seems that our human nature desires to demonstrate to the world how badly we have been treated. So we add the two things together. First the death, and then the bad back. After that, it is only too easy to add to the list every single negative thing that takes place in life.

Selwyn Hughes as a counsellor has wide experience of the kind of depression, inward-looking mentality and spiritual dis-ease that is caused by this kind of 'adding up'.

The path to spiritual health is through ensuring that our mental list is one of blessings and good things, rather than set-backs and bad things.

Questions to consider

- Is your personality one that is naturally drawn to positive thoughts, or do you find the lesson in this chapter hard to learn?

....

....

- The man in the story on pages 43–45 had his perspective changed by seeing others much worse off than himself. Would that work for you?

  _____

  _____

  _____

  _____

- What one thing, more than any other, makes your heart well up in gratitude to God?

  _____

  _____

  _____

  _____

THE ATTITUDE OF GRATITUDE

Are you a natural 'thank-er'? Do you always send a thank you note after a meal out? Do you write thank you letters after Christmas? Have you ever sent letters such as those described on page 47 – notes of appreciation to those who have helped you or encouraged you in life?

There is no doubt that depression and misery make us inward looking. And when we get into that state it is very difficult to think of others and to imagine how they feel. It is difficult, too, to turn our hearts in gratitude and thankfulness to our heavenly Father for all His blessings and goodness to us.

Imagine a small boy. It is about eight weeks before Christmas. The boy wants a bicycle for Christmas, and he begins to drop hints. 'I *really* would like a bike. All my friends have got one. Dad, you used to have a bike when you were young. Why can't I have one?'

And so it goes on, week after week, until Christmas morning arrives. There, at the end of the bed, is a shiny new bicycle – just what he wanted. Does the boy say, 'Well, what a coincidence! I was hoping for a bike!' No! He runs into his parents' room and throws himself into their arms. 'Thank you! Thank you! It's wonderful!'

The difference between the two lies in the relationship between the boy and his father. He knows that his request has been heard, that his father loves him and has chosen the best for him. And so he runs to offer his thanks. (And his father will probably ensure that he sits down and writes thank you letters for all his other Christmas presents, too!)

Questions to consider

- How often do you take time to '*notice the hand of God*' in your life (Charles Spurgeon, p.46)? Is thankfulness a part of your daily prayer time?

....

....

....

- *'The Almighty often sends His special blessings by way of people and I think He likes His agents to be thanked also'* (p.48). Do you regularly thank the people who bring God's blessings into your life?

....

....

....

....

CHOOSE TO BE THANKFUL

It is often the case that those Christians who have grown up in the Roman Catholic Church, or in the higher churches of the Anglican communion, understand much better the necessity for living by the will, rather than by feelings.

As Selwyn Hughes says on page 51, people will sometimes label as hypocrisy the offering of worship or prayer when we don't 'feel like it'.

In his book *A Long Obedience in the Same Direction* (IVP), Eugene Peterson says:

We can act ourselves into a new way of feeling much quicker than we can feel ourselves into a new way of acting. Worship is an act that develops feelings for God, not a feeling for God that is expressed in worship.

So, you are having a bad day. Lots of small problems. Your plans didn't work out. The sun didn't shine. Your feelings have taken a slide. You look, act and feel grumpy. What are you going to do?

Are you going to compose a negative list, and reel it off to your family on your return home? Or are you going to do as the psalmist did in Psalm 103, and charge your soul to praise the Lord? '*He is saying, in effect, I am going to use my will to stir up my mind to focus on reasons why I should praise the Lord. I may not feel like doing it but I am going to do it anyway!*' (p.51).

Scripture is full of incidences when the people of God were reminded of God's blessings. How many times, I wonder, does the phrase 'who brought you out of Egypt' occur? A wonderful, stupendous act of God, which resulted in freedom and the beginning of a new life. What better way to deal with grumpiness than to remember something fantastic?

Questions to consider

• Is there an incident in your life that just thinking about makes you feel better? Perhaps your conversion, or a miracle of healing?

- *'You can trace every good and perfect gift to the Father above'* (p.55). Are there good things in your life that you have never really thanked God for?

GIVING THANKS IN EVERYTHING

Many years ago, a book was published in this country which divided Christians into two camps. Merlin Carothers' *Prison to Praise* was an impassioned plea to the people of God to praise Him in everything. But some people found it impossible to praise God for cancer, or road accidents, or disaster. They could trust God for His help, and thank Him for it, but they could not praise Him for the problem itself. That felt like blasphemy.

Take a few moments to re-read the story of Corrie ten Boom on page 60. Then remind yourself of the story of Joseph in Genesis chapters 37–45. Standing outside the situation, we can see the hand of God. From inside, it's a different story.

There may be something in your life right now that seems to you to be anything but a blessing. But *'No matter what happens to you God is committed to working good out of it and because of that it is possible to thank Him for everything that happens to you'* (p.59). Our belief in the goodness of God may begin with His mercies to us in conversion and provision, but it will grow as we see Him at work in the disasters and the problems. Just think: every Sunday you join with others in thanking God that His Son, Jesus Christ, suffered a horrible death. Why? Because you know the stupendous things that death achieved in the purposes of God. *'If you start there then I promise you it won't be long before you begin to develop a right response to all the setbacks of life. You will find yourself saying, even in the most difficult of circumstances, "Thank You, Lord, for letting this happen. I can't wait to see how You are going to turn it to good"'* (p.59).

Questions to consider

- Is there something in your life that you find it difficult to thank God for? Can you imagine how it might turn out in a way that would demonstrate His love and concern for you?

- How would you help someone who is going through a difficult time, and who felt that God was far away?

ACTION PLAN

- *'You might be better off adopting Sir John Templeton's approach by lying quietly in your bed after you have awakened and thinking of five new ways you have been blessed'* (p.42). Keep a notebook by your bed, and use it to record the good things that God gives you.

- *'I think He likes His agents to be thanked'* (p.48). Think of three people who have been influential in your life, and write letters of thanks to them.

- *'It's sad when Christians wait until they feel like praising rather than using their wills to command their minds to focus on reasons for praise'* (p.52). Plan into your prayers definite times when you thank God for the *common* blessings, the *special* blessings, and the *spiritual* blessings He has given you (p.54).

- *'The world is flooded with bad news'* (p.45). How might your church ensure that prayer times have a right balance between thanksgiving and supplication?

- *'We forget the good things God has done for us'* (p.53). In your family, plan regular times to think back and remember God's blessings. Use photograph albums, family videos and other reminders of happy times.

Law 3

KEEP ON KEEPING ON

"It is a law of the soul that those who keep on keeping on and never give up will find their souls fortified for the task. They will not only find a reward waiting them at the end but they will experience the blessing of God on the way to that reward" (p.68)

PERSEVERANCE

Have you noticed how hard it is these days to find people prepared to take on long-term commitments? It has become almost impossible to find leaders for the uniformed youth movements like Scouts and Guides. It is difficult to find people prepared to take on a Sunday school class or to help with church cleaning. Why is this?

You will find a clue to the answer if you spend any time watching television. In the soap operas, for example, listen out for the words, 'It's not working out, is it?' Marriages are dissolved, partnerships brought to an end, relationships die, jobs are thrown up. The moment difficulties arise, the answer is to get out. If at first you don't succeed – give up. That's the motto of the culture we live in.

But in this chapter, Selwyn Hughes draws us away from the world's attitudes, and fixes our attention on the Scriptures, and the need for perseverance. As the quote from John Stott says, '*We must resist the intellectual and moral pressure of our contemporary world and refuse to conform to the fashions of the day*' (p.69).

Spend a few moments looking up the references quoted on pages 68–69. Then take a look at the letters to the churches in Revelation 2 and 3, with their exhortations to faithfulness and perseverance, and their promises to those who 'overcome'. Soak your mind in these verses and pray that God will give you the strength to persevere.

Questions to consider

- Looking at the story of Winston Churchill (pp.66–67), how would you define the difference between stubbornness and perseverance?

\
\
\
\

- How would you describe your own record of perseverance? Are you a stay-er, or do you quickly give up on things and move on?

\
\
\

THE REASONS PEOPLE GIVE UP

Selwyn Hughes, with his great experience in counselling, has talked with and helped many people with their problems, and he is therefore not afraid to look those problems in the face and to tackle them in the light of Scripture and the promises of God.

Unfortunately, the evangelist Selwyn Hughes quotes on page 71 is not unique. There are still those who assure their congregations that good health and prosperity are our right as children of God and inhabitants of the kingdom of heaven. However, as Selwyn Hughes reminds us, Jesus in John 16:33 says differently: *'In this world you will have trouble …'*

> *Why do people fail to be steadfast and persevere? Why do they defect? This is an issue that has exercised me greatly over the years. My research into this subject has revealed that in the main those who fall by the way do so for four reasons.*
> *1. They become discouraged by reason of trials and troubles.*
> *2. They are unable to deal with doubts about the faith.*
> *3. They are overcome by persecution from others.*
> *4. They fall into sin and do not know how to rise again.*
>
> (p.70)

The following questions look at these four main reasons why believers fail to persevere in the faith. Together with another Christian, spend a few minutes asking the Holy Spirit to help you work through these, and to bring into the light any areas of weakness or potential failure. Then pray for one another, that God will provide you with *'the inner strength to persevere and overcome every obstacle that confronts [you]'* (p.72).

Questions to consider

- Trials and trouble
  'Life is more tragic than orderly' (Oswald Chambers, p.70). Have you experienced tragedy in your life? How did it affect your belief and faith in God?

- *'Life is not just something to be enjoyed but rather is a task that each one of us is assigned'* (p.71). Do you believe this? Do you see problems as 'tasks' from God, or as interruptions to your fellowship with Him?

- *'Unmerited suffering is a problem for many'* (p.71). Imagine the young woman whose children died (p.71) is in your church. How would you go about helping her?

- Doubts about the faith
  What aspects of Christian belief have you ever had doubts
  about? How did you deal with your doubts?

- '*Satan is a tempter. The art of doubting is natural to us in our
  fallen condition, but Satan often works on our doubts and tempts
  us to unbelief*' (p.74). Have you blamed yourself for your slide
  into unbelief? Can you see how your doubts might have been
  worked on by Satan?

- Persecution
  Have you experienced hostility or mockery for your faith? How did you deal with it?

- When you fall into sin
  Have you ever been so ashamed of something you have done, that you were ready to give up the Christian life (p.80)? How did you deal with that?

- 'The real problem was the lack of firm moral resolve' (p.81). How can you strengthen your moral resolve so that you can avoid sin?

RUN THE FULL RACE

There is all the difference in the world between the amateur and the professional. St Paul's three examples to Timothy in 2 Timothy 2 – the soldier, the athlete and the farmer – show up that difference most dramatically. Training, discipline and more discipline are what make a soldier, not a uniform. Training, discipline and more training, are what make an athlete successful, not the latest sportswear. Experience, hard work and more hard work are what bring the farmer's rewards, not a new tractor.

It's the long haul that is important. We need to know where we are going to draw our strength from in the long term. Today's church meeting may have been inspiring and encouraging, but the glow will fade, and reality will be there when we wake tomorrow morning.

Packer suggests that the secret of recovering your spiritual footing at a time when everything is falling around you lies in the little word 'think'.

Doubtless David would have focused his mind on God. And that is the secret we must learn, to keep our minds on Him – His greatness, His power and, above all, His ability to bring good out of everything. (p.85)

Questions to consider

- *'I'm giving it everything I've got'* (1 Cor. 9:26, *The Message*; p.83). Can you honestly say that you are giving the Christian life 'everything you've got'?

- On page 85, Selwyn Hughes imagines how David might have gone about finding strength in God. What helps and encourages you to persevere?

ACTION PLAN

- *'Never give up'* (p.67).
  Is there an area of your life where you are conscious of having 'given up'? What one thing could you do to begin to put things right?

- *'The soul will not flourish simply by going to church, singing a few hymns and thinking your Christian duty has been done'* (p.69).
  How good is your church at encouraging members in their daily lives? How might support be offered to those going through difficult times?

- *'So many Christians complain of spiritual doubt while all the time they do not use the secret weapon'* (p.76).
  How much do you read the Bible? Be honest! What could you do to increase your knowledge of God's Word?

- *'He ... centred his thoughts on the promises that God had made to him'* (Jim Packer, p.85).
  Is there a promise of God that is very special to you? How can you use that to help you persevere in difficult times?

- *'Don't give up. If God has called you to do something then make sure you finish it. Struggle is the chrysalis out of which a new vision of God comes. When pressure comes against you, persevere. God will not let you down. You will find that His strength is more than a match for anything you are called to face'* (p.86).
  Make a list of the things you do for God: your job, caring for your family, teaching in Sunday school, and so on. Then write down

    (a) what might cause to you give up on that task; and

    (b) how you can find the strength to persevere.

Law 4

REMEMBER TO FORGET

"It is another law of life, I believe, that spiritual health and success depend on our ability to forget the hurts and injuries that others have given us – not to have them erased from memory, but to deal with them in such a way that we are not emotionally overwhelmed by them." (p.91)

THE POWER TO FORGET

*P*recious though a good memory is, the power to forget is
equally precious. Henri Gergson, the French philosopher,
said, 'It is the function of the brain to enable us not only to
remember but also to forget.'

   Much of the time I have spent in helping people with their
problems over the years has been focused on helping people forget.
This is because so often when I have encouraged people to let go
of the past with all its hurts and painful memories and to forgive
those who have hurt them they have responded by saying, 'I can
forgive but I can't forget.' They forgive but they don't want the
other person to forget they have forgiven (p.89).

Sometimes, when people are involved in road accidents, they
find that the last few seconds before the impact, and the moment of
the accident itself, are a complete blank. The brain has 'edited out'
something too painful and traumatic to remember.

   Others, however, remember in startling detail all the
circumstances that led up to the incident, and they play it over and
over again in their waking and sleeping moments. They are haunted
by the trauma for weeks or months afterwards.

   We have no control over such responses. We either live with the
blank in our minds; or we learn to cope with the memories. But we
can't decide which.

   In this chapter, Selwyn Hughes makes it absolutely clear that in
our Christian lives, we *do* have a choice. We have to decide whether

we will we allow the mercy of God to help us forget injury and hurt, or go over and over it in our minds, keeping alive the sense of pain and injustice.

'*One cannot of course forget the facts; it is the bitterness and the emotional overwhelming from which deliverance may be found*' (p.92). That is the key to this chapter. We can't choose to forget an incident or a harsh word or action. It happened, on such-and-such a day, at such-and-such a time. It happened. Nothing will change that. But the pain, the unhappiness, the hurt, the bitterness – those we can be delivered from. Hallelujah!

Questions to consider

- '*I can forgive but I can't forget*' (p.89). Do you sympathise with this response? Have you ever said this?

- Have you ever been '*emotionally overwhelmed*' (p.91) by some hurt or injury – to yourself or someone you love? How did you deal with it?

• *'Forgiveness is a wonderful idea until we have someone to forgive'* (C.S. Lewis, p.95). Why do you think we find forgiveness so hard?

AS YOU HAVE BEEN FORGIVEN

There is one cry, common to all mankind, from Adam in the Garden of Eden, to the small child growing up in the twenty-first century: 'It's not fair!' Somehow, deep inside each of us is the idea that life ought to be just, with goodness rewarded, wrong punished and virtue recognised and revered.

So when we suffer (as we think) unjustly, or when we are hurt or injured without having first inflicted hurt ourselves, we hate the unfairness of it all. 'He started it!' 'Well, you brought the subject up!' 'It was self-defence, officer!' 'It wasn't my fault!'

But something happens to our values and our ideas when we become Christians. We move into another dimension, another kingdom, where goodness goes on being good, even when crucified. Where peace operates in the middle of a violent storm. Where love never ends, but goes on and on forgiving wrong.

'*The longest journey in the world, it has been said, is the eighteen inches between the head and the heart*' (p.101). And there lies our problem. We may be well taught in the Christian life, and have read the story of the unmerciful servant in Matthew 18:21–35 many times, but until our hearts are truly touched by the amazing fact of God's forgiveness, we won't be freed from that striving for what the world calls justice.

Questions to consider

- '*When people say to me, "My problem is I can't forgive." I say, "No, that is not your problem. Your problem is you don't know how much you have been forgiven*' (p.97). How strong is your sense of the forgiveness of God?

- '*At that point Peter got up the nerve to ask, "Master, how many times do I forgive a brother or sister who hurts me? Seven?"… When Jesus replied, "Seven! Hardly! Try seventy times seven" … He is suggesting an infinite number of times*' (pp.98–99).
Is there a situation in your life where you find it hard to go on forgiving? Why is that?

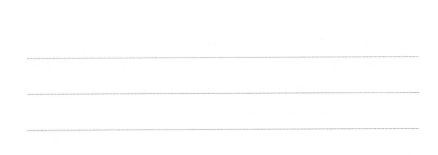

THE CONSEQUENCES OF NOT FORGIVING

From the story of Adam and Eve onwards, the Scriptures are full of dramatic incidences of people getting their come-uppance. The ground opened and swallowed them up. Or their children were killed. Or the nation was overwhelmed and sent into exile. Even in the New Testament we read how Ananias and Sapphira died as a result of their sin, and Paul writes to the church at Corinth that sin is the reason many have become sick and died.

But such drama is not part of our everyday lives. We discover that a respected church leader has been having an affair for many years. But nothing happens. He may leave the church and set up somewhere else, but no thunderbolts fall on him. His children still flourish. His garden still blooms.

And so we may be led into thinking that the spiritual principle of cause and effect no longer operates. Times have changed. Our culture is more accepting. Everyone is entitled to live the way they choose.

But read again Selwyn Hughes' words on page 106: '*The consequence of not forgiving is deeply serious. I can't tell you the number of people I have met in my time who bore all the marks of having been handed over to the torturers; they had become old before their time, wizened, dried up.'*

There really is no doubt about it. The issue of lack of forgiveness is one that carries with it consequences that cannot be avoided. Get down on your knees now, and ask God to help you.

Questions to consider

- 'The sin of unforgiveness ... takes its terrible toll upon us now' (p.104). Do you agree with Selwyn Hughes' interpretation? Have you known bitterness and hate as a result of not being able to forgive someone?

- Do you identify with the testimony of the doctor on page 105? Have you been *'striving unconsciously to pay back the debt'*?

ACTION PLAN

I believe there are three things necessary in order to forgive and forget.

First, focus on how much you have been forgiven. *Think how extensive God's mercy has been in your life. You may think you have committed only little sins but, as someone has put it, there are no little sins, just as there is no little God to sin against ...*

Secondly, deal honestly with any lingering resentments that may be in your soul. *This is always a challenging moment. No doubt some of you reading these lines will have gone through deep hurts and even deep horror. As you think now of that person who hurt you, abused you, slandered or libelled you, tortured you, rejected you, release the poison of bitterness in Jesus' name. Let it gush out before God and tell Him that you want to be free ...*

Thirdly, ask God to help you forget. *If you accept the responsibility to forgive then God will accept the responsibility to help you forget. You can bank on it. You do the possible, God will do the impossible. It's as simple as that.* (pp.106–109)

- '*Surely you are not sending a Christmas card to* him?' (Sangster, p.88). Is there anyone you have 'crossed off your list' because of some hurt they have done you? Ask God to show you one thing you could do to begin the process of forgiveness and reconciliation.

- *'How many churches split over little issues that ought to be forgotten, instead of being the cause of one group going off in a different direction, fractured, splintered and a monument to failure?'* (p.92). Are there any issues in your church right now which threaten to divide the fellowship? Apply Psalm 119:165 to that situation, and begin to pray daily for peace and reconciliation.

- *'Focus on how much you have been forgiven'* (p.106). Make a list of any sins you are conscious of, and which you have confessed and asked forgiveness for. Spend some time deliberately thanking God for His grace in forgiving you those things.

- *'Deal honestly with any lingering resentments'* (p.108). Write down the names of any people against whom you feel resentment of any kind. Begin to include a daily prayer for them, and ask God to release you from bitterness against them.

- *'Ask God to help you forget'* (p.109). Find a prayer partner who will pray regularly with you and for you, that God will enable you to 'remember to forget' hurts and injuries in the past.

Law 5

GIVE YOURSELF
TO OTHERS

Gy

"The law ... of being more interested in others than in

oneself – is called in Scripture the law of love.

The apostle James calls it 'the royal law'" (p.117)

IMPROVE YOUR SERVE

With the enormous sociological changes in the world in the last hundred years, many of us in the West don't really know what a servant is. The untouchables of India, the cotton-picking slaves of America, the despised scullery maid of Victorian England: these are simply figures in history books.

Companies encourage the lowliest of employees to become shareholders, and so enjoy the right to have a say in the running of the business. In offices and organisations across the world, secretaries are expected to work their way up through the company and become managers in their own right.

The figure wrapped in a towel and washing His friends' feet is totally alien to our culture. And anyway, what does 'foot-washing' mean to ordinary people with family commitments and full-time jobs in the twenty-first century?

Selwyn Hughes directs our thinking first to the very nature of the Trinity, and the relationship between Father, Son and Holy Spirit (p.115). He tells how considering that relationship, and how it is expressed, caused a profound change in his life and ministry.

Pray now that the Holy Spirit will enable you to understand what D. Broughton Knox calls the '*essence of reality*', and how it can change the way in which you think and act.

Questions to consider

• How much do you identify with the experience of Arthur Gordon (p.112)? Has your life so far made you self-centred?

• *If you don't share of yourself in some way or another then you demean yourself. Something within shrivels up and your zest for life will diminish* (pp.113–114).
  Do you agree that without service to others, something within us 'shrivels up' (p.114). Why do you think that is?

• Have you ever experienced a *'paradigm shift'* (p.114) in your own life? What happened?

THE LAW OF LOVE

The supermarket is crowded with shoppers. Everyone is trying
to get through the checkouts as quickly as possible, but one aisle
is blocked. A young mother is desperately trying to restrain and
quieten a small boy. He is screaming, kicking, throwing himself on
the floor and generally letting go in a big way. Some onlookers smile
at the mother in sympathy. Others click their tongues in disapproval
of her lack of discipline. Most simply shrug their shoulders and
remember battles with their own children during the 'terrible twos'.

But what makes small children so prone to tantrums? Is it not
that their parents are trying to train them to look away from self, and
to consider other people? We come into this world already infected
with the '*congenital illness*' of Adam (p.124), and we fight against the
instructions to share our toys, to say thank you, to offer the biscuits
round first. The story of the little boy and his goldfish on page 125
captures exactly the essence of self-interest that is the hallmark of
the human race.

> *Whenever I think of how easily self-interest can arise in our hearts,*
> *my mind goes back to a story I heard my father tell. A little boy*
> *came home from school one day to discover his pet goldfish lying*
> *stiff and motionless on the surface of the goldfish bowl. He was*
> *devastated and began to cry.*
>
> *His father tried to console him by saying: 'It's sad when a pet*
> *dies, but here's what we will do. We'll put the dead little fish in a*
> *matchbox, take it out into the garden and invite your friends to*
> *join with us in conducting a funeral service. Then afterwards I*

will take you and your friends to the ice cream parlour and buy you all an ice cream.'

The little boy was cheered by this promise but suddenly he noticed that the goldfish was not dead as he had supposed, but had revived somehow and begun swimming merrily around the bowl. The little boy gave a whoop of joy, and clapped his hands in glee that his pet goldfish was still alive.

A few minutes later, however, he remembered the promise of his father to take him and his friends to the ice cream parlour. Now that would no longer be a possibility and he had mixed emotions – gladness that his goldfish was still alive, but sadness that he would miss out on a trip to the ice cream parlour. Eventually one emotion dominated the other and turning to his father said, 'Let's kill it.' (p.125)

Most of us grow to adulthood with the ability to wear a veneer of politeness and consideration, and our self-interest shows itself only in the 'acceptable' forms of competitiveness, ambition or our keenness to be in authority over others.

Once we become Christians, however, we have to face up to the reality of our own sinfulness and selfishness. Reading the testimonies of Eugene Peterson (p.122) and Selwyn Hughes himself (p.116), we can be encouraged that we are not alone in our battle against self. Others have gone before us, and discovered the spiritual law that if we want to be like Jesus, then we must learn to give ourselves to others in love.

Questions to consider

• What would you say is the main way that self-interest demonstrates itself in your life?

_____

_____

_____

_____

• *'To love is to be vulnerable'* (C.S. Lewis, p.121). Have you been hurt in the past by those you have tried to love? How did you deal with that?

_____

_____

_____

_____

LEARNING TO SERVE

Did you seen the television programme where the life of a large country house in Edwardian times was reconstructed. The house itself was equipped with furnishings, lighting and heating as it would have been, and members of the public were asked to come and play the parts of family, friends and servants.

How revealing it was to eavesdrop on the conversations in the servants' hall, where they battled with their feelings at having to consider the family as their 'betters', and to do the most menial jobs without any thanks. These were people who had chosen to take part, and who, when the programme was over, would go back to their own lives. But still they found it almost impossible to knuckle down and bear the indignity of living as servants.

Spend some time reading through the scriptures on pages 132 and 133, and see how different you are meant to be.

Questions to consider

- *'In a room where nobody saw / And nobody knew'* (p.129). Why do you think it is so difficult for us to be loving and giving when no one knows about it?

- *'Do nothing out of selfish ambition or vain conceit, but in humility consider others better than yourselves. Each of you should look not only to your own interests, but also to the interests of others. Your attitude should be the same as that of Christ Jesus'* (Phil. 2:3–5)

What do you think it really means to 'consider others better than yourselves'?

_____

_____

_____

_____

ACTION PLAN

- *'If one's motives are wrong nothing can be made right'* (Arthur Gordon, p.113).
  List three things that you do (eg a job, a church commitment, a family responsibility) and ask God to help you assess the motives you have for doing those things.

- *'One way we can protect ourselves from being hurt is to refuse to be vulnerable, to steel ourselves against other people and stop loving them'* (p.121)
  Is there someone you have stopped loving because of the hurt they have caused you? Before God, decide on one thing you can do to begin to love again.

- *'The Servant King'* (p.126). Deliberately set aside some time to read through Mark's Gospel. Ask the Holy Spirit to reveal to you Jesus, the Servant King, and how you can follow His example.

- 'Not so with you. Instead, whoever wants to become great among you must be your servant ...' (Matt. 20:26). How can your church ensure that leaders – house group leaders, worship leaders, youth leaders – understand the principle of servanthood?

- 'Begin to think of ways in which you can minister to others in love' (p.133). What practical thing might you do in the next few days to begin to bless others and show them God's love?

> *Tilt your soul in the direction of serving rather than being served, of giving rather than receiving. Develop an attitude of giving. All actions begin with the right attitude. Everyone has their favourite scripture and this is the one, which I quoted before, that I turn to regularly:*
>
> *Do nothing out of selfish ambition or vain conceit, but in humility consider others better than yourselves. Each of you should look not only to your own interests, but also to the interests of others.*
> *Your attitude should be the same as that of Christ Jesus:*
> *Who, being in very nature God,*
> *did not consider equality with God something to be grasped,*
> *but made himself nothing,*
> *taking the very nature of a servant,*
> *being made in human likeness.*
>
> Phil. 2:3–7 (pp.133–134)

Law 6

STAY CLOSE TO GOD

Sc

"Where there is no genuine repentance there can be no ongoing and developing relationship with God." (p.142)

THE WAY IN

Probably the best illustration of true repentance is still Jesus' story of the Prodigal Son in Luke 15. Selfish, greedy, impatient and profligate, a young man lives to please only himself. Until one day, with his money gone, his friends gone and himself an outcast he 'came to his senses' (Luke 15:17). What he does at that point is to decide to go back, to return (re-turn).

He goes, with no expectation of welcome or reinstatement, but only a desire to be once again a member of his father's household. The amazing outcome of his return is, of course, his father's welcome, the complete reinstatement as son, and the celebration feast.

Earlier in the same chapter, Jesus had already explained, twice, the joy that pervades heaven when a sinner repents, when the lost are found, and this story emphasises it again. So we can be absolutely sure of our own welcome when we begin to put the principles of this chapter into action. On the day of your conversion, heaven went wild with joy. And every time you come back and repent, whether it be of major sin, or of wrong attitudes, lack of love or selfishness, there is another party in heaven.

No one says it's going to be easy. The struggle of the butterfly to escape its cocoon (p.141) is a hard one. But read again those three stories in Luke 15 before you embark on this chapter, and listen for the cheering of the angels!

Questions to consider

- '*He found himself in the throes of repentance – the spiritual revolution that takes place in the soul when one begins to realise one's need to find forgiveness for sin and turn one's life over to God*' (p.139). How big a part did repentance play in your own conversion?

- Which of the three stories in Luke 15 do you most identify with: the sheep that has strayed away, the coin that lies hidden and lost, or the rebellious child?

A NEW VIEW

Have you ever been in a room and noticed someone, or a group of people, on the other side? For a moment you observe them, dispassionately, wondering who they are. And then with a sudden shock, you realise that you are looking into a mirror, and what you are seeing is yourself and your own family or friends.

Usually the moment is too short to allow any detailed observation, but you might have thought fleetingly that the person in the mirror was fat, or old, or dressed in the wrong colour, or looking miserable. But all too quickly the impression fades, and you return to your own inbuilt ideas about who you are and how you look.

James tells us that the Word of God is a mirror (James 1:22–25). It shows us clearly what we are and what we look like in the sight of God. And only those who take action as a result of what they see will be blessed by God.

As Selwyn Hughes takes us through the meaning and importance of repentance, a mirror will be held up to you. Do you want to go on being the person in the mirror, or do you want to do something about it? You might receive a bit of a jolt as you catch sight of yourself in a mirror and think yourself old or fat, but what will happen when you see your soul in the Word of God will be more like an earthquake.

> 'Repentance,' says Dr John White, 'is a changed way of looking
> at things' [Changing on the Inside, *Eagle Publishing*]. *He*
> *defines repentance as the shock that comes from seeing reality.*
> *It is a terrible thing to claim to be a Christian and yet to live*
> *independently of the life offered to us in Christ, to relegate God to*
> *irrelevance. The full realisation of that, brought about by the Holy*
> *Spirit, can, says John White, be like an earthquake in the soul.*
> *Without this inner revolution, this earthquake in the soul, nothing*
> *deep and profound happens in a person's spiritual life.* (p.143)

Questions to consider

- *'Suddenly I felt naked and unclean'* (Charles Colson, p.143). Have you ever had an experience like this? What caused it? How did you respond?

-

-

-

-

- *'Repent and be baptised'* (Acts 2:38). How important do you think the act of baptism is in the process of repentance?

-

-

-

-

THE WAY TO LIVE

One of the lessons artists and designers have to learn is the law of perspective: things in the distance look smaller. In the theatre, you might 'cheat' the audience into thinking there is a long street on the stage by placing street lamps from the front to the back, tall at the front, and gradually reducing in size to the back of the stage. *Et voilà!* It looks like a long street.

Perspective is how you see things from where you are standing. If you stand in a different place, then things will look different. So, if you are standing in the wings of the stage, you will see the street lamps as they really are.

This whole question of repentance is also a matter of where you stand. There is an old hymn which includes the words:

Those who fain would serve thee best
Are conscious most of wrong within.

It seems that the nearer we are to God, the more our view of ourselves will change; we can no longer 'cheat' ourselves into thinking that we are anything but weak, needy and quite incapable of pleasing Him.

'*Repentance … is also a daily attitude, a perspective*' (Colson, p.146). As you study this part of Selwyn Hughes' chapter on repentance, be prepared to move to a different place, so that you can see yourself as you really are. And then you need to make sure that you stand in that place every day of your life.

In John 13, Jesus said to His disciples, 'A person who has had a bath needs only to wash his feet.' You may indeed have repented fully at your conversion, but daily contact with the world, daily challenges to your love of self, daily attacks from the enemy will mean that you need to have Jesus 'wash your feet'.

Questions to consider

- How would you explain to a new Christian, unfamiliar with Scripture, what it means to 'abide in Christ' (John 15:4–8).

  ....

  ....

  ....

- On pages 147 and 148 Selwyn Hughes describes some of the things that took the place of Christ in his life. What are your 'other lovers'?

  ....

  ....

  ....

  ....

- *'Repentance [is] … a kind of death'* (p.155). How can we embrace something that is so against our human nature?

  ....

  ....

  ....

ACTION PLAN

- Having read through this chapter, is there something you believe
  you need to repent of? Read through Selwyn Hughes' prayer of
  repentance on page 149, and then write your own, listing the
  things that you truly want to turn away from.

- '*Repentance is not regret. Regret is being sorry for oneself ...*
  Repentance is not remorse. Remorse is sorrow without hope at its
  heart ...
  Repentance is not reformation. Reformation ... may follow
  repentance, but it can never precede it.
  Repentance is not reparation. Reparation ... is practical proof of
  the reality of repentance ...' (p.141).
  Spend some time studying these four words and what they
  mean, and how they differ from true repentance.

- '*We do men and women a disservice when we try to make it easy*
  for them to enter the Christian life' (p.142). Do you think this is
  true in your church? What can you do to ensure that the need for
  repentance is made clear?

- What steps can you take to avoid living in '*a state of nervous*
  tension' (p.158)?

- Plan into your daily times alone with God a period of
  confession. Make a 'check list' of the things which you have
  identified in your study of this chapter, and ask the Holy Spirit
  to help you turn away from sin daily.

Law 7

CULTIVATE YOUR SOUL

Cs

"The truth is, of course, that like many things in this world success comes when God and man team up. Though God is the one who designed the soul, it requires care and husbandry on the part of the human being who possesses it, if it is to grow and develop in the way it should.

If the worship of God is the first law of the soul, then most certainly the cultivation of it is an important law also. If it isn't cultivated then it will degenerate and die!" (p.160)

THE CULTIVATION OF THE SOUL

The first thing that Almighty God did after the work of creation, and His day's rest, was to plant a garden. The Creator of the earth was so pleased with His creation that He moved around it, choosing this plant, and that tree, and that shrub. He rejoiced in the beauty and fruitfulness of the earth, celebrating it in a lovely garden.

And down through the ages He has used the lessons of the vine and the fig tree, the rose and the cedar, the seed and the harvest, to teach His children the lessons of His kingdom.

Selwyn Hughes too, in this final chapter, uses an analogy drawn from the worlds of horticulture and agriculture: and speaks of the necessity of cultivating the soul. Unfortunately, we humans are often content with exactly the way things are, and we have no desire to start clearing the ground, ploughing up the earth and planting what our heavenly Father wishes to grow.

We prefer the crop of blackberries that appears as a result of letting the hedges run wild, and we love the colour of the yellow ragwort that invades the fields. We like to see the bindweed winding its way around every plant in our garden, and we don't realise until too late that the choice we have made leads to degeneration and death.

Any farmer will tell you that cultivation is hard work. So as you come to this final chapter, you will need to be prepared to buckle down. As someone once said:

A garden is a lovely thing,
But gardens are not made

By saying, 'Oh how beautiful!'
And sitting in the shade.

Questions to consider

* *When we turn to the Bible and ask ourselves the question, what is the soul? we get the best answers. Although there are many connotations to the word (and Bible writers didn't seem to give precise technical definitions to words like 'heart', 'mind' and 'soul'), the word appears to have two distinct meanings – life and personality (p.163).*
How much do you think about your soul?

  ....

  ....

  ....

  ....

* *'When [the soul] comes into the kingdom it has the feeling of coming into its own'* (p.164). Did you experience this sense of homecoming and comfort on your conversion?

  ....

  ....

  ....

  ....

THE DISEASE OF THE SOUL

Do you want to know the difference between influenza and a cold? Imagine a £50 note on the lawn outside your house. You look down from your bedroom window and see it. If you decide to go down and pick it up, you only have a cold. If you decide you can't be bothered, not even for £50, then you have the flu!

Sickness of the soul is one that cannot be seen by others, but like the flu it can paralyse us and make any change too great an effort to contemplate. We may be playing our part in an active church, teaching or leading, joining in worship or serving others. But we know that something is wrong. Selwyn Hughes uses the word 'degeneration'.

The law of degeneration runs through the whole of creation. If we neglect our body it will rapidly deteriorate. If it is the mind we neglect then it will degenerate into imbecility. If the conscience, it will run off into lawlessness and vice.

With this law or principle staring us in the face the words of the writer to the Hebrews rise almost to cosmic proportions:

For if the word spoken through angels proved steadfast, and every transgression and disobedience received a just reward, how shall we escape if we neglect so great a salvation, which at the first began to be spoken by the Lord, and was confirmed to us by those who heard Him.

Heb. 2:2, NKJV

If we neglect the usual means of keeping a garden in order how shall it escape turning to weeds? If we neglect the soul how shall it escape dissolution and death? (p.166).

While others seem to grow in grace and love, we seem to be getting further and further behind: *'The power that pulls us down, lowering us, blinding reason, searing conscience, paralysing the will'* (p.168).

And the cause? Simply neglect.

If you think that your soul is degenerating, rather than growing, then now is the time to take action. Resolve to neglect it no longer.

Questions to consider

- *'Experience shows that we will shape ourselves further into sin … unless we expend some energy and effort to move against it'* (p.166). Has this been your experience? Is there an area of your spiritual life which continues to deteriorate?

- *'The Christian life is a way of living and not merely a decision once made'* (p.168). How different is your 'way of living' from those who are not believers, and who have not made that decision?

THE ANTIDOTE

Often, when we need to understand an abstract concept like the soul, it is the poet who is able to help us the most. By using imagery and words that spark ideas and thoughts in our minds, poets can help us make sense of the unseen world.

In Psalm 1, David paints a picture of those who are blessed by God, those who are cultivating their souls. He tells us that they are like trees planted by the water's edge. Of course, any analogy breaks down at some point: in this case, a tree cannot actually decide where to plant itself. But, as Selwyn Hughes explains in this final section of his book, we can so decide. We can decide that we *will* spend time with God; we *will* read His Word regularly; we *will* learn how to listen to Him and pray to Him.

> *For years now, a conviction has been growing in my heart that the Christian life rises and falls at the point of the devotional – those times when one meets privately with the Lord to deepen one's intimacy with Him. There the soul becomes at its best* (p. 172).
>
> *The quiet time … shuts you in with God, the door closes upon you and then infinite resources begin to bubble up from beneath and you are lifted up. The door opens and you glide out onto a higher level of life. You will be surprised – and other people will*

too – at how easily you transcend worries and fears and difficulties and seem to live life on a higher level. It's the result of being shut in with God.

That's the power of the quiet time – the place where the soul grows best. (p.182)

As we saw earlier, the work of cultivation is hard work, but the river of the life of God is available for us to draw on. The Holy Spirit is ready and waiting to lead us into all truth. And we have His promise that, if we do undertake this work of cultivation, '*whatever we do will prosper*' (Psa. 1:3).

ACTION PLAN

- '*The nurse of full-grown souls is solitude*' (James Russell Lowell, p.171).
  How often are you able to be alone with God? Plan to increase the amount of time, and to give that time priority in your day.

- '*Read your Bible*' (p.176).
  Can you think of three ways in which you could increase the quantity and quality of your Bible reading?

- '*Listen to God*' (p.178).
  Resolve to buy and read the book quoted on page 179, and to give time to learning how to listen for the voice of God.

- '*Pray*' (p.180).

  Start a notebook in which to record specific prayers (and their answers!).

- '*Salvation in its broadest sense is salvation from the downward bias of the soul. It takes in the whole process of rescue from the power of sin and selfishness that goes on all the time in our lives, the power that pulls us down, lowering us, blinding reason, searing conscience, paralysing the will.*' (pp.167-168).

  What steps can your church take to ensure that new Christians are taught how to enter fully into salvation, and how to 'cultivate their souls'?

Congratulations on finishing this workbook. Come back to it on occasions and we promise you that you will discover, with the Holy Spirit's help, new insights and new understanding.

NATIONAL DISTRIBUTORS

UK: (and countries not listed below)
CWR, Waverley Abbey House, Waverley Lane, Farnham, Surrey GU9 8EP.
Tel: (01252) 784700 Outside UK (44) 1252 784700

AUSTRALIA: CMC Australasia, PO Box 519, Belmont, Victoria 3216.
Tel: (03) 5241 3288 Fax: (03) 5241 3290

CANADA: David C Cook Distribution Canada, PO Box 98,
55 Woodslee Avenue, Paris, Ontario N3L 3E5. Tel: 1800 263 2664

GHANA: Challenge Enterprises of Ghana, PO Box 5723, Accra.
Tel: (021) 222437/223249 Fax: (021) 226227

HONG KONG: Cross Communications Ltd, 1/F, 562A Nathan Road, Kowloon.
Tel: 2780 1188 Fax: 2770 6229

INDIA: Crystal Communications, 10-3-18/4/1, East Marredpalli, Secunderabad
– 500026, Andhra Pradesh. Tel/Fax: (040) 27737145

KENYA: Keswick Books and Gifts Ltd, PO Box 10242, Nairobi.
Tel: (02) 331692/226047 Fax: (02) 728557

MALAYSIA: Salvation Book Centre (M) Sdn Bhd, 23 Jalan SS 2/64, 47300
Petaling Jaya, Selangor. Tel: (03) 78766411/78766797 Fax: (03) 78757066/78756360

NEW ZEALAND: CMC Australasia, PO Box 303298, North Harbour,
Auckland 0751. Tel: 0800 449 408 Fax: 0800 449 049

NIGERIA: FBFM, Helen Baugh House, 96 St Finbarr's College Road,
Akoka, Lagos. Tel: (01) 7747429/4700218/825775/827264

PHILIPPINES: OMF Literature Inc, 776 Boni Avenue, Mandaluyong City.
Tel: (02) 531 2183 Fax: (02) 531 1960

SINGAPORE: Alby Commercial Enterprises Pte Ltd, 95 Kallang Avenue #04-00,
AIS Industrial Building, 339420. Tel: (65) 629 27238 Fax: (65) 629 27235

SOUTH AFRICA: Struik Christian Books, 80 MacKenzie Street, PO Box 1144,
Cape Town 8000. Tel: (021) 462 4360 Fax: (021) 461 3612

SRI LANKA: Christombu Publications (Pvt) Ltd, Bartleet House,
65 Braybrooke Place, Colombo 2. Tel: (9411) 2421073/2447665

TANZANIA: CLC Christian Book Centre, PO Box 1384, Mkwepu Street,
Dar es Salaam. Tel/Fax: (022) 2119439

USA: David C Cook Distribution Canada, PO Box 98, 55 Woodslee Avenue,
Paris, Ontario N3L 3E5, Canada. Tel: 1800 263 2664

ZIMBABWE: Word of Life Books (Pvt) Ltd, Christian Media Centre,
8 Aberdeen Road, Avondale, PO Box A480 Avondale, Harare.
Tel: (04) 333355 or 091301188

For email addresses, visit the CWR website: www.cwr.org.uk
CWR is a Registered Charity – Number 294387
CWR is a Limited Company registered in England – Registration Number
1990308

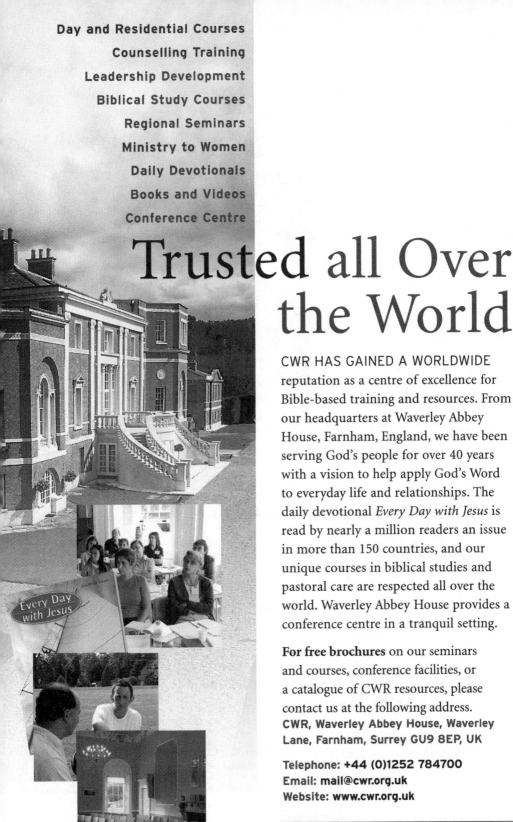

Day and Residential Courses
Counselling Training
Leadership Development
Biblical Study Courses
Regional Seminars
Ministry to Women
Daily Devotionals
Books and Videos
Conference Centre

Trusted all Over the World

CWR HAS GAINED A WORLDWIDE reputation as a centre of excellence for Bible-based training and resources. From our headquarters at Waverley Abbey House, Farnham, England, we have been serving God's people for over 40 years with a vision to help apply God's Word to everyday life and relationships. The daily devotional *Every Day with Jesus* is read by nearly a million readers an issue in more than 150 countries, and our unique courses in biblical studies and pastoral care are respected all over the world. Waverley Abbey House provides a conference centre in a tranquil setting.

For free brochures on our seminars and courses, conference facilities, or a catalogue of CWR resources, please contact us at the following address.
CWR, Waverley Abbey House, Waverley Lane, Farnham, Surrey GU9 8EP, UK

Telephone: **+44 (0)1252 784700**
Email: **mail@cwr.org.uk**
Website: **www.cwr.org.uk**

 Applying God's Word
to everyday life and relationships

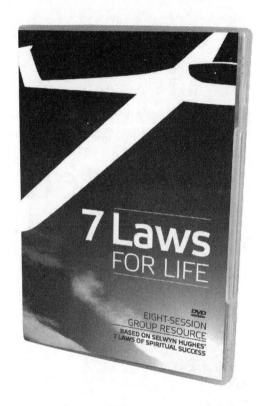

7 Laws for Life DVD

If you enjoyed this book, why not share its insights with your church or small group, using our DVD?

It makes the seven laws come to life in a memorable and exciting way.

Eight deeply challenging, 20-minute sessions are presented by CWR's Mick Brooks in various locations including a maze, a police cell and a glider!

EAN: 5027957001114
Only £19.99 (plus p&p)

Prices correct at time of printing

For the first time, Selwyn Hughes' *7 Laws of Spiritual Success* is available complete with its companion workbook, *Applying the 7 Laws of Spiritual Success*, in one volume. The 7 Laws of Spiritual Success teaching was regarded by Selwyn as his legacy to the next generation.

We often contrast Old Testament 'law' with New Testament 'grace', believing that law has now made way for a forgiving relationship with Father God. So, you might wonder why an author well-known for his passionate belief in God's mercy and forgiveness wrote a book all about laws.

In his many years of Christian ministry, Selwyn discovered that there are key elements in the Christian life that are more than mere principles. As reliable as the laws of nature, he discovered laws of Christian living which, when followed, enable us to live successful lives. *7 Laws of Spiritual Success* is a refined presentation of Selwyn's most potent observations.

Jennifer Oldroyd's excellent workbook, included in this edition, contains much to encourage and challenge the Christian trying to apply this life-giving teaching. She takes us through Selwyn's teaching step by step, and provides probing questions and practical action plans perfect for either group or individual study.

UK PRICE: £9.99

www.cwr.org.uk

ISBN 978-1-85345-468-4

9 781853 454684

Tel: 01252 784700
Email: mail@cwr.org.uk

CWR Applying God's Word
to everyday life and relationships

CHRISTIAN LIFE